SOMETHING TO BOAST ABOUT

UNCOVERING
AND MEETING
EVERY PERSON'S
GREATEST NEED
OF THE HEART

MIKE BROWN

Author: Mike Brown
Published by: OneHope Publishing
Printed by: CreateSpace, an Amazon.com company
Available on: Amazon.com, CreateSpace.com and other retail outlets

Heartfelt appreciation is expressed to Cheryl Brown, Leanne Phelps and Sherrie Davidson for their significant support in proofreading and editing this book.

Cover design: Mike Brown

Scripture Permissions

Scripture quotations marked (ESV) are taken from the ESV® Bible (The Holy Bible, English Standard Version®), copyright © 2001 by Crossway, a publishing ministry of Good News Publishers. Used by permission. All rights reserved."

Scripture quotations marked (NIV2011) are taken from the Holy Bible, New International Version®, NIV®. Copyright © 1973, 1978, 1984, 2011 by Biblica, Inc.™ Used by permission of Zondervan. All rights reserved worldwide.

Scripture quotations marked (NKJV) are taken from the New King James Version®. Copyright © 1982 by Thomas Nelson. Used by permission. All rights reserved.

Copyright 2018 – Mike Brown

All rights reserved under international copyright law. Permission is granted to copy exerts from this book for non-profit usage, not exceeding 600 words, so long as such copy does not violate the scripture copyrights.

ISBN 978-0-9976300-3-9

Scripture Formatting
To make this book as readable as possible, scripture text is included in the book text. Scriptural quotations are indented and italicized to clearly identify them, like this:

> Matthew 15:18 (NIV2011)
> *18 But the things that come out of a person's mouth come from the heart, and these defile them.*

Words or phrases of scripture quoted as part of the commentary text are italicized without quotation marks, like this: '. . . the created heavenly hosts. He is called a *covering cherub* or *guardian cherub*. He stood at the very throne of God.'

Other Books by this Author:

❖ Celebrating God's Purpose for the Ages
Drawing Nearer to the God of Origin and Eternal Destiny Through Bible Prophecy, an extensive cross-reference commentary on prophecy from Genesis through Revelation as it relates to the big picture of redemption (2016 2nd edition, paperback 440 pages, available on Amazon, ISBN-978-0-9976300-0-8)

❖ The Mysterious Magi of Christmas
Renewing the Christmas Mystique by Distinguishing the Biblical from the Traditional, an exploration of this story's role in the wide scope of God's purpose (2016 paperback 40 pages, available on Amazon, ISBN-978-0-9976300-1-5)

❖ The Vision of the Patriarchs
Messages to Us from Revealed Insights of the Hebrew Pioneers, bridging the time-gap between the patriarchs and us and connecting with the grand purpose of redemption in devotional application style (2017 paperback 65 pages, available on Amazon, ISBN- 978-0-9976300-2-2)

CONTENTS

	Page
Preface	1
1. A Personal Perspective of Boasting	2
2. What God Says About Boasting	7
3. Things to Not Boast About	14
4. Something to Boast About	34
5. The God we Boast Of	50
6. Other Things Worth Boasting About	64
7. Becoming Boasters	70

PREFACE

This book uses the avenue of boasting to explore the state and structure of the human 'heart' from a biblical perspective. It investigates the anatomy of human motivation. It unmasks attempts at self-righteousness and offers, instead, an alternative approach to true righteousness.

What things are you most proud of? What things do you regret? The Bible speaks widely about boasting. It gives specific areas of boasting that are offensive to God. Perhaps surprisingly, it also offers areas in which boasting is encouraged. Gathering truth about this subject from throughout the Bible, Old Testament and New, this book then leads us into God's self-revelation to our self-centered souls. This topic of boasting leads us into the realm of knowing and pleasing God. We will find that God is a seeking, revealing, relational God. You will see that He is seeking you. You will encounter a saving, redeeming God.

If you are not a believer, but have an open mind, I invite you to consider the timeless wisdom of scripture. Today, the Christian Bible is routinely disparaged by a large sector of our American culture and around the world. In spite of its being constantly attacked and ridiculed, it remains the largest selling book in print. It is by far the most influential of all books ever written. There is a reason for that, which you will learn here. Instead of following the crowd's ear-stopping suppression of its message, why not see if the biblical truths presented here speak to your heart and intellect.

Mike Brown

Chapter 1
A PERSONAL PERSPECTIVE OF BOASTING

We think little about it when we see a professional football player follow a touchdown with a dance recital. All that is lacking is tights and a tutu. That seems normal and typical now. Things seem to have changed significantly during my lifetime. I was born in 1949. I grew up with the notion that excessive boasting was socially unacceptable. I don't know exactly when and where I learned that lesson. I'm sure my parents trained me in that regard, and it also soon became evident that people spoke disparagingly of and ridiculed those who bragged too much. No doubt, it was a learning process. By whatever means, I learned that excessive boasting was socially obnoxious, and was a turn-off for acceptability and popularity.

I am not suggesting that I never struggled with egotism, as everyone does, showing itself in various combinations of pride and inferiority. Of course, I struggled to attain a place in the pecking order of my peers that at least did not make me an outcast. I actually remember praying to God as a child that I was not seeking greatness, but please just make me normal. I don't know why that childhood prayer lingers in my memory, but it does and it now seems relevant, if not significant. Yet, while I was not immune to ego-related issues, I did learn to somewhat cover them up publicly.

Thus, the sub-culture in which I grew up seemed to support a more humble outward appearance. Then in 1964, during my ninth grade year, something happened that shattered my view of that culture. A monumental match was staged for the world heavyweight boxing championship. Sonny Liston, the defending champion, was very heavily favored over newcomer Cassius Clay. Liston's thunderous punches had terminated most of his fights with first or second round knockouts. Many upcoming fighters declined to fight him for fear of being destroyed. Clay, the upstart young guy, stunned the sports world by upsetting Liston with a knockout of his own. Clay (later renamed Mohammad Ali) went on to defend that title over a long career. From before that fight until after his fighting days faded, Clay was very outspoken, blustery and braggadocios. I watched in amazement as he stood before the TV cameras after that fight, beating his chest and yelling repeatedly into the microphone, "I'm the greatest! I'm the king!" I remember thinking that his arrogance would surely villainize him. With the media, it did just that, at first. But something surprising occurred. Many in the general public loved his antics and jumped on his bandwagon of popularity. I was more amazed at the reaction of the public than by his show of egotism.

I am not enough of a social scientist to know if that incident was influential in a shift of the cultural norm or simply a manifestation of it. I can say that it was my first remembered experience of blatant arrogance being applauded rather than detested by the public. It shocked my boyish ideals when it did not turn out the way I expected.

Now, I realize that for many of you reading this, that incident and this issue seems somewhat insignificant, somewhat irrelevant. The reason it doesn't seem unusual is that in today's culture this type of behavior is common in the sports world. You may not be old enough for this to seem too abnormal. At that time it seemed extremely 'across the grain' with the prevailing society I thought I had somewhat figured out. So now, after a touchdown, it is normal to see a theatrical display and, in college football, penalties for excessive celebration are common. The penalties are not really about celebration, but about curbing the overt public display of arrogance as being 'unsportsmanlike.' Many teams and coaches alike are expected to not only play with confidence, but to carry themselves on and off the field with "swagger." That word is commonly used to describe the arrogant, boastful demeanor expected of today's athletes. Swagger is the attitude of our time in athletics. It is another name for arrogance.

This current trend is not limited to sports. It shows itself in politics, business and countless other arenas. It has become much more than just an adopted behavior. It seems intrinsic to the identity of many of today's up-and-coming generation.

My assessment is that such arrogance is still recognized by a majority of people as disgusting, rather than admirable. Most people are still annoyed by excess boasting, seeing it as displaying a lack of intelligence or character in the person doing it. But annoyed as we might be, we are not surprised by it. Our sensibilities to it have been dumbed down by its prevalence in today's culture.

Who Decides?

Given this social divide regarding arrogant, boastful behavior, who should make the rules; who should set the standard? If we turn to public opinion for a consensus on the matter of boasting, we enter the realm of morality, seeking what is suggested as the mores of society. We are seeking to know, 'What is acceptable?' Of course, the answer to that will always be, 'Whatever we, collectively as a society, want it to be.' The realm of ethics, on the other hand, asks the question, 'What should be acceptable?' It sees a standard that supersedes the opinion of a certain segment of our culture, be it majority interest, special interest, or personal interest.

Besides public opinion, there might be many other venues for seeking opinion. The problem with them all is they lack authority in the matter. Who cares about their opinion except those who seek acceptance from special interests or isolated peer groups.

However, there is One who has the authority to govern in this matter. God has a lot to say about it and has done so in his written word, the Bible. God will be our authority and the Bible will be our source for considering this matter. I won't attempt a systematic defense of the inerrancy and adequacy of scripture. There are many books available to do that, and that is not within the scope of this book. I simply begin this study from the perspective of the Bible being our adequate and only pertinent source.

The Root of the Issue

What is the problem with boasting? Is it really a problem, or is it just a socially annoying habit? Frankly, when I hear excessive boasting, I am often amazed that the person doing it seems blind to their own behavior. Is it a root problem, or a festering of a deeper, more serious problem?

This will be revealed to us as we search the scriptures, but yes, boasting is a manifestation of a bigger, more pervasive issue. It stems from a flawed perspective of one's ego, signaling either inflated pride or a sense of inferiority. Even the inferiority motive is really an expression of pride. Pride, regardless of how it manifests itself, is at the heart of boasting. All of us are vulnerable to pride in one way or another. That is why pride is such a significant issue. Our pride is exposed in our boasting. It is a window into the heart of a person. Jesus taught this.

> *Matthew 15:18 (NIV2011)*
> *[18] But the things that come out of a person's mouth come from the heart, and these defile them.*

> *Luke 6:45 (NIV2011)*
> *[45] A good man brings good things out of the good stored up in his heart, and an evil man brings evil things out of the evil stored up in his heart. For the mouth speaks what the heart is full of.*

Boasting is a manifestation of pride, the more fundamental problem. Thus, we speak of boasting and pride as nearly synonymous. Boasting is simply an outward expression of the priorities and motives of the proud heart. Boasting is not the only manifestation of pride, but it is one of the more overt and visible ones.

General Scriptural Aspects of Boasting
Scripture makes literally hundreds of statements about ego-related issues. Let's just pick out a few samples. For one thing, arrogance and boasting are contrary to true love.

> *1 Corinthians 13:4 (ESV)*
> *[4] Love is patient and kind; love does not envy or boast; it is not arrogant*

True love is focused on another. When we are swollen with pride, loving ourselves rather than anyone else, then we are not acting in love.

Furthermore, arrogant pride is said to be characteristic of the rise of evil in society during the last days.

> *2 Timothy 3:1-5 (ESV)*
> *[1] But understand this, that in the last days there will come times of difficulty. [2] For people will be lovers of self, lovers of money, proud, arrogant, abusive, disobedient to their parents, ungrateful, unholy, [3] heartless, unappeasable, slanderous, without self-control, brutal, not loving good, [4] treacherous,*

> reckless, swollen with conceit, lovers of pleasure rather than lovers of God, [5] having the appearance of godliness, but denying its power. Avoid such people.

Not that there haven't been such people and behavior in every age, but in the last days the world at large will be typified without restraint by these attributes. Notice that in this 2 Timothy passage scattered among what we might consider more serious crimes such as *abusive, brutal and treacherous,* we find maladies of the ego: *proud, arrogant, swollen with conceit.* This shows us the seriousness and prevalence of this condition, a condition described metaphorically by the psalmist.

> *Psalm 73:6 (ESV)*
> [6] *Therefore pride is their necklace; violence covers them as a garment.*

Pride and boasting are symptoms of a life that is self-centered. We all are naturally self-centered people, so the message of God's perspective on this issue is pertinent to us all. Overt arrogance signals a deep-seated pride that closes God out of one's sphere of influence. God is not included in that person's thinking. Without godly influence, a person is vulnerable to many other vices as well. Thus, we see boasting as an outward festering of an inward and potentially disastrous condition. It is not about the external, although we talk a lot about that. It is primarily about our hearts.

While the title of this book suggests the theme is about boasting, it is really about recognizing and training our natural self-centered focus to become focused toward God and others. In other words, having a heart of humility, which pleases the Lord. I have heard it said that 'if we think we are humble, we aren't.' That implies that humility is something that imperceptibly comes over us, and with which we have no initiative. I disagree. I believe that humility is a constant battle, but one for which we can be trained. We train ourselves over time by growing in our knowledge of God and of ourselves. We gain that knowledge and understanding from sustained reading, studying, and applying scripture to our lives. Therefore, humility can be developed, albeit imperfectly, in this life.

Chapter 2
WHAT GOD SAYS ABOUT BOASTING

The Beginning of Pride
If pride is such a serious sin, where does it come from; how did it originate in a world created by a holy God and deemed by Him to be *good*? The earliest manifestation of pride revealed to us in scripture occurred sometime prior to Genesis 3, the fall of mankind. God tells us something of it through the mouths of his prophets.

> *Isaiah 14:12-15 (NKJV)*
> *[12] "How you are fallen from heaven, O Lucifer, son of the morning! How you are cut down to the ground, You who weakened the nations! [13] For you have said in your heart: 'I will ascend into heaven, I will exalt my throne above the stars of God; I will also sit on the mount of the congregation On the farthest sides of the north; [14] I will ascend above the heights of the clouds, I will be like the Most High.' [15] Yet you shall be brought down to Sheol, To the lowest depths of the Pit.*

> *Ezekiel 28:16-17 (NIV2011)*
> *[16] Through your widespread trade you were filled with violence, and you sinned. So I drove you in disgrace from the mount of God, and I expelled you, guardian cherub, from among the fiery stones. [17] Your heart became proud on account of your beauty, and you corrupted your wisdom because of your splendor. So I threw you to the earth; I made a spectacle of you before kings.*

Lucifer was the most glorious of all the created heavenly hosts. He is called a *covering cherub* or *guardian cherub*. He stood at the very throne of God, guarding or attending to God's holiness. Then pride entered the picture and, as a result, there was treason and rebellion in heaven.

> *Revelation 12:7-9 (NIV2011)*
> *[7] Then war broke out in heaven. Michael and his angels fought against the dragon, and the dragon and his angels fought back.*
> *[8] But he was not strong enough, and they lost their place in*

heaven. ⁹ *The great dragon was hurled down—that ancient serpent called the devil, or Satan, who leads the whole world astray. He was hurled to the earth, and his angels with him.*

Human Pride

Thus, we have the earliest biblical mention of pride and how it became motivation in the mind of Satan. Satan wasted little time enlisting Adam and Eve in his rebellion. In the book of Romans, Paul describes man's own insurgence. Notice how simply it began.

Romans 1:21-23 (NIV2011)
²¹ For although they [mankind] knew God, they neither glorified him as God nor gave thanks to him, but their thinking became futile and their foolish hearts were darkened. ²² Although they claimed to be wise, they became fools ²³ and exchanged the glory of the immortal God for images made to look like a mortal human being and birds and animals and reptiles.

It began by men and women neglecting to give God glory and thanksgiving. They became self-absorbed, a natural result of pride. If you research a secular description of man's religious experience, you will likely find it taught that human life began without any awareness of God. As his evolving mind became more intelligent, he began asking profound and obvious questions such as, "How did I get here?" and "How is it that I am so amazingly designed for life?" Then man developed religious thoughts to try to answer these questions. This describes how religion started, according to humanistic secularists. This passage from Romans contradicts that theory head-on. According to scripture, man began with a knowledge of his Creator, but chose to focus only on himself, and to marginalize God. This led to idolatry, immorality, violence, and every other evil practice.

Pride is at the forefront of evil, and it throws up a roadblock for communion with our Creator. In one Old Testament example, King Uzziah changed from doing what was right before God to doing evil in His sight, all because of his pride.

2 Chronicles 26:16 (ESV)
¹⁶ But when he was strong, he grew proud, to his destruction.

For he was unfaithful to the LORD his God and entered the temple of the LORD to burn incense on the altar of incense.

The ravages of pride showed themselves at every level of the culture of the chosen nation and from earliest times until later in their history. God showed his hostility toward their proud hearts by condemning them and by bringing calamity on the people. Old Testament scripture condemns the proud in the biblical books called 'wisdom literature':

Job 35:12 (ESV)
[12] There they cry out, but he does not answer, because of the pride of evil men.

Psalm 31:23 (ESV)
[23] Love the LORD, all you his saints! The LORD preserves the faithful but abundantly repays the one who acts in pride.

Proverbs 15:25 (ESV)
[25] The LORD tears down the house of the proud but maintains the widow's boundaries.

Proverbs 8:13 (ESV)
[13] The fear of the LORD is hatred of evil. Pride and arrogance and the way of evil and perverted speech I hate.

Proverbs 11:2 (ESV)
[2] When pride comes, then comes disgrace, but with the humble is wisdom.

Proverbs 16:18 (ESV)
[18] Pride goes before destruction, and a haughty spirit before a fall.

Proverbs 21:24 (ESV)
[24] "Scoffer" is the name of the arrogant, haughty man who acts with arrogant pride.

Proverbs 29:23 (ESV)
[23] One's pride will bring him low, but he who is lowly in spirit will obtain honor.

> *Psalm 94:2 (ESV)*
> ² *Rise up, O judge of the earth; repay to the proud what they deserve!*
>
> *Proverbs 16:19 (ESV)*
> ¹⁹ *It is better to be of a lowly spirit with the poor than to divide the spoil with the proud.*

Old Testament prophecies also cast judgment on the proud, such as in our theme passage from Jeremiah 9:23-24, and in this one:

> *Isaiah 2:11-12 (ESV)*
> ¹¹ *The haughty looks of man shall be brought low, and the lofty pride of men shall be humbled, and the LORD alone will be exalted in that day.* ¹² *For the LORD of hosts has a day against all that is proud and lofty, against all that is lifted up—and it shall be brought low;*
>
> *Isaiah 57:15 (NIV2011)*
> ¹⁵ *For this is what the high and exalted One says— he who lives forever, whose name is holy: "I live in a high and holy place, but also with the one who is contrite and lowly in spirit, to revive the spirit of the lowly and to revive the heart of the contrite.*

In this last passage, we see the magnanimous character of the Lord, high and exalted, but also drawing near to the person of low spirit and penitent in heart. God is in glory and at the same time also in intimate nearness to the humble. What a magnificent revelation about God!

Likewise, the New Testament casts a shadow of judgment on pride:

> *James 4:6 (ESV)*
> ⁶ *... Therefore it says, "God opposes the proud, but gives grace to the humble."*
>
> *1 Peter 5:5-6 (ESV)*
> ⁵ *Likewise, you who are younger, be subject to the elders. Clothe yourselves, all of you, with humility toward one another, for "God opposes the proud but gives grace to the humble."*

> *⁶ Humble yourselves, therefore, under the mighty hand of God so that at the proper time he may exalt you,*

As already discussed in chapter 1, Jesus, when being questioned by the religious leaders about eating food without ceremonially cleansing it, had this to say.

> *Mark 7:20-23 (ESV)*
> *²⁰ And he said, "What comes out of a person is what defiles him. ²¹ For from within, out of the heart of man, come evil thoughts, sexual immorality, theft, murder, adultery, ²² coveting, wickedness, deceit, sensuality, envy, slander, pride, foolishness. ²³ All these evil things come from within, and they defile a person."*

Notice the list includes *envy, slander, pride* in the same listing with what we might consider more serious sins of defilement. The central message of Jesus in this passage is that pride and its offshoots envy and boasting, along with a host of other sins, are evidence of the depravity of the fallen human heart from where they originate. The prophet Jeremiah proclaimed this message from the Lord:

> *Jeremiah 17:9-10 (NKJV)*
> *⁹ "The heart is deceitful above all things, And desperately wicked; Who can know it? ¹⁰ I, the LORD, search the heart, I test the mind, Even to give every man according to his ways, According to the fruit of his doings.*

Other translations render the phrase *desperately wicked* to read *desperately sick* and *beyond cure*. One version translates the phrase *Who can know it* by the phrase *Who really knows how bad it is*, which makes the 'not knowing' as not about not understanding the heart, but rather about not comprehending the depth of the heart's depravity. The bottom line of all this is that the natural human heart is full of evil, and the extent of that evil defies our understanding. Additionally, we learn that the person is powerless to escape from this condition in and of himself or herself.

> *Romans 3:19-20 (NIV2011)*
> *¹⁹ Now we know that whatever the law says, it says to those who are under the law, so that every mouth may be silenced and the*

whole world held accountable to God. [20] *Therefore no one will be declared righteous in God's sight by the works of the law; rather, through the law we become conscious of our sin.*

We cannot clean up our act and earn our way into God's grace. The Law of God, that is—the Old Testament commandments—was not given as a path to righteousness because no one is able to keep it. Rather, the commandments were given to open our eyes to our own condition. The path they take us on is a path of condemnation. They are given to bring us to hopelessness and helplessness. That is the starting point toward humility. Once we come to a place of surrender, a place where there is no way out, then we are ready to meet with God.

Next, it reminds us who makes the call. We cannot justify ourselves by comparing ourselves with someone else. Rather, we are reminded that in the final analysis, God sets the criteria for righteousness. He alone will pass judgment on how we measure up. In fact, He has already passed judgment on us. Here is what he concluded; here is His verdict:

Romans 3:10-12 (NKJV)
[10] *As it is written: "There is none righteous, no, not one;* [11] *There is none who understands; There is none who seeks after God.* [12] *They have all turned aside; They have together become unprofitable; There is none who does good, no, not one."*

What are we to do? God declares that we are hopeless and helpless. That is very troubling, or it should be. That is His message to all of mankind, to every last one of us. It is catastrophic unless God Himself intervenes in our behalf. Salvation begins when we surrender ourselves to God; when pride is replaced by defeat. Then we are on the brink of becoming humble, a condition about which God says *I live in a high and holy place, but also with the one who is contrite and lowly in spirit.* That condition of utter futility is what prompted Jesus to say,

Matthew 5:3 (NIV2011)
[3] *"Blessed are the poor in spirit, for theirs is the kingdom of heaven.*

The *poor in spirit* are declared to be *blessed* because they are now at a point where they are desperate for God's mercy. They have surrendered any attempt at self-righteousness. Boasting is exterminated. The humble heart is ready to embrace its Savior. That Savior is Jesus. Jesus paid the price for our sins by his death on the cross and by his resurrection. We must come to that cross helpless and hopeless and receive the sacrificial love that God has poured out to us.

Thus, we see that pride is much more than just a social malfunction. God classifies it a very grievous sin. A condemning sin. Boasting is a symptom of that pride. By God's grace in sending Jesus to us, we see an escape from the penalty and practice of that sin and from all sin.

Strangely perhaps, there are certain topics and certain circumstances in which boasting is spoken of in scripture as being appropriate. In the following chapters, we will investigate a biblical distinction between things to not boast about and things that we should boast about. In the meantime, please bear with the opening negative perspective. It is as valuable as the positive for knowing the mind of the Lord.

Chapter 3
THINGS TO NOT
BOAST ABOUT

Before you conclude from the last chapter and from the title of this one that this book is too negative, please know that we are taking things in the order in which they appear in our theme scripture text. So bear with us as we seek to learn something of the spiritual anatomy of the human heart before going on to more positive things.

In this chapter we introduce the main theme scripture passage for this book. It will define not only the book's message, but also its structure, as well. We will begin to see some specifics about what God says about pride, arrogance and boasting and to pursue His guidance of what to boast about and not to boast about.

The Old Testament prophet Jeremiah prophesied in Judah just before and during the Babylonian invasion led by Nebuchadnezzar of the Chaldeans. This invasion was brought on by God's providence, as punishment for Israel's unfaithfulness. Israel had become marked by national self-pride. God allowed the wicked Babylonians to invade, plunder and exile the chosen nation as punishment for their idolatry, violence, immorality and indifference towards God. Much of the book of Jeremiah is either a prophecy of judgment or a lament over Israel's condition.

In the midst of one of the prophetic discourses foretelling of the impending invasion and destruction, we encounter a stand-alone statement that is truly ageless in its application. This short passage seems to leap out of the historical context to teach us some universal life principles. It is a definitive statement about pride and boasting. It is so fundamental that its principles and words are reflected in other prophecies, in the psalms, and it is quoted or referred to multiple times in the New Testament. The time has come to introduce this passage as the theme scripture for this book. This book is written as a commentary on this passage.

Jeremiah 9:23-24 (ESV)
[23] *Thus says the LORD: "Let not the wise man boast in his*

*wisdom, let not the mighty man boast in his might, let not the rich man boast in his riches, *[24]* but let him who boasts boast in this, that he understands and knows me, that I am the LORD who practices steadfast love, justice, and righteousness in the earth. For in these things I delight, declares the LORD."*

In this passage, we are given a hierarchy of human endeavor from God's perspective. Wisdom, strength and wealth are given to people in varying degree. They are often achieved largely through human effort. When a person does possess one of these, there is a natural tendency to display it as personal achievement. Even these earthly endeavors are a gift from the Lord. Not all who seek and work for them gain them. Even those things we work for and attain are gifts because God gives the ambition and intellect to pursue and achieve them. People naturally pursue those things that bring satisfaction. His or her ability to achieve those goals, or lack of ability to achieve them, can soon lead to either pride or shame. Pride or shame then draw one into selfishness and away from the knowledge of God. The psalmist spoke of pride as part of this three-fold rebellious nature of fallen man.

Psalm 10:3-4 (ESV)
[3] For the wicked boasts of the desires of his soul, and the one greedy for gain curses and renounces the LORD. [4] In the pride of his face the wicked does not seek him; all his thoughts are, "There is no God."

Notice in this Psalm passage the three areas of application: *desires, greedy* and *pride*. Notice how they correspond with the three realms of influence against which our theme passage speaks. Human pride and arrogance is offensive to God. It represents a self-centeredness that pushes God to the periphery or completely out of mind.

In this chapter, we will focus on the three natural human motivations in which we are not to boast—those introduced in the passage by the phrase *let not*. These three areas represent three realms of human endeavor. They define three realms of temptation. They are not intended for just some people. They potentially characterize and motivate every one of us.

As Christians, we are regularly made aware in scripture of our dependency on God's mercy and grace. We have nothing to boast about because our salvation comes from Him. The right to it comes from Him. The means of attaining it comes from Him. The reward of it is from Him.

> *Ephesians 2:8-9 (ESV)*
> [8] *For by grace you have been saved through faith. And this is not your own doing; it is the gift of God,* [9] *not a result of works, so that no one may boast.*

In our theme passage, we are given three areas of behavior that commonly engender boasting of ourselves: 1) human wisdom, 2) might or strength, and 3) riches or possessions. These arenas represent three realms of motivation that beset humans. It is amazing how frequently they show up in scripture either separately or grouped together. Perhaps the clearest statement about these realms as a group is found in John's first letter.

> *1 John 2:15-16 (NKJV)*
> [15] *Do not love the world or the things in the world. If anyone loves the world, the love of the Father is not in him.* [16] *For all that is in the world—the lust of the flesh, the lust of the eyes, and the pride of life—is not of the Father but is of the world.*

Here John differentiates things *of the world* from things *of the Father*. The world is that realm in which we live; in which our mortal desires motivate us to do our own will. Jesus said we cannot *serve two masters*, satisfying our own desires while simultaneously following after God. Thus, the world fights against our spiritual well-being constantly. As John used the term *world*, Paul used the term *flesh* to signify our mortal life with its motives and desires when he wrote:

> *Romans 8:5-9 (NIV2011)*
> [5] *Those who live according to the flesh have their minds set on what the flesh desires; but those who live in accordance with the Spirit have their minds set on what the Spirit desires.* [6] *The mind governed by the flesh is death, but the mind governed by the Spirit is life and peace.* [7] *The mind governed by the flesh is hostile to God; it does not submit to God's law, nor can it do so.* [8] *Those who are in the realm of the flesh cannot please God.*

⁹ You, however, are not in the realm of the flesh but are in the realm of the Spirit, if indeed the Spirit of God lives in you. And if anyone does not have the Spirit of Christ, they do not belong to Christ.

When we live in the world, we not only battle against our own sin nature; we are also influenced by outside temptations. Paul's word *world* and John's word *flesh* refer to our realms of temptation as mortal humans. Paul and John both employ strong language to describe the effect of natural (worldly or fleshly) living on one's relationship with God.

The trilogy of worldly motivation (*lust of the flesh, lust of the eyes and pride of life*) first showed itself when Satan tempted Eve. Note those same three realms of temptations he attacked.

Genesis 3:6 (NIV2011)
⁶ When the woman saw that the fruit of the tree was good for food and pleasing to the eye, and also desirable for gaining wisdom, she took some and ate it. She also gave some to her husband, who was with her, and he ate it.

When the woman saw that the fruit of the tree was good for food refers to lusting *of the flesh. And that it was delightful to the eyes* makes obvious reference to the *lust of the eyes.* The *pride of life* is seen in her thoughts expressed by the phrase *and that the tree was to be desired to make one wise.*

In another example, after the angel Gabriel announced to Mary that she was going to give birth to the Son of God, she visited her near relative Elizabeth in another town. In their spirit-filled greeting she broke out in praise in what has become known as 'Mary's Song.' Note this portion of it.

Luke 1:51-53 (ESV)
⁵¹ He [God] has shown strength with his arm; he has scattered the proud in the thoughts of their hearts; ⁵² he has brought down the mighty from their thrones and exalted those of humble estate; ⁵³ he has filled the hungry with good things, and the rich he has sent away empty.

Verse 51 speaks of the prideful, verse 52 addresses the *mighty* and verse 53 condemns the love of riches. This is a clear reference to these three areas of self-aggrandizement.

When Jesus was tempted in the wilderness after his baptism, we see this same three-pronged approach by Satan.

> *Matt 4:2-3,5-6,8-9 (NIV2011)*
> *² After fasting forty days and forty nights, he was hungry. ³ The tempter came to him and said, "If you are the Son of God, tell these stones to become bread." . . . ⁵ Then the devil took him to the holy city and had him stand on the highest point of the temple. ⁶ "If you are the Son of God," he said, "throw yourself down. For it is written: " 'He will command his angels concerning you, and they will lift you up in their hands, so that you will not strike your foot against a stone.'" . . . ⁸ Again, the devil took him to a very high mountain and showed him all the kingdoms of the world and their splendor. ⁹ "All this I will give you," he said, "if you will bow down and worship me."*

God turned these areas of temptation into avenues of victory when Jesus was crucified and rose from the dead. Notice how Paul addresses the three realms

> *1 Corinthians 1:27-31 (ESV)*
> *²⁷ But God chose what is foolish in the world to shame the wise; God chose what is weak in the world to shame the strong; ²⁸ God chose what is low and despised in the world, even things that are not, to bring to nothing things that are, ²⁹ so that no human being might boast in the presence of God. ³⁰ And because of him you are in Christ Jesus, who became to us wisdom from God, righteousness and sanctification and redemption, ³¹ so that, as it is written, "Let the one who boasts, boast in the Lord."*

Foolish/wise, weak/strong, things that are not/things that are. Again, we see these three topics: the pride of life, the lust of the flesh and the lust of the eyes, in that order. This is an obvious reference to our theme passage, from which he quotes. These areas of temptation aim at getting us to put trust in created things rather than the Creator. They entice us to focus on temporal things rather than eternal things. They coerce us into disobedience. They are the strategies of Satan. But Jesus gives us victory over these things through his atoning sacrifice. We are delivered from God's wrath against man's rebellion when we embrace God's substitutionary atonement of Jesus for our sins. Paul notes that man initially knew God, but chose otherwise.

> *Romans 1:18-23 (NIV2011)*
> *[18] The wrath of God is being revealed from heaven against all the godlessness and wickedness of people, who suppress the truth by their wickedness, [19] since what may be known about God is plain to them, because God has made it plain to them. [20] For since the creation of the world God's invisible qualities—his eternal power and divine nature—have been clearly seen, being understood from what has been made, so that people are without excuse. [21] For although they knew God, they neither glorified him as God nor gave thanks to him, but their thinking became futile and their foolish hearts were darkened. [22] Although they claimed to be wise, they became fools [23] and exchanged the glory of the immortal God for images made to look like a mortal human being and birds and animals and reptiles.*

We are called to make choices continually based on where our allegiance and affection lies, either with God or with the ways of the world. The two are diametrically opposed to each other. Paul wrote to the Colossians, reminding them of this war for their affection.

> *Colossians 3:1-6 (NIV2011)*
> *[1] Since, then, you have been raised with Christ, set your hearts on things above, where Christ is, seated at the right hand of God. [2] Set your minds on things above, not on earthly things. [3] For you died, and your life is now hidden with Christ in God. [4] When Christ, who is your life, appears, then you also will appear with him in glory. [5] Put to death, therefore, whatever belongs to your earthly nature: sexual immorality, impurity, lust, evil desires and greed, which is idolatry. [6] Because of these, the wrath of God is coming.*

Let's visit each of these three areas of worldly motivation and temptation more closely, the realms that are destined for God's wrath, to see what else the Bible has to say about them.

The Lust of the Flesh

Some translations render this "desires of the flesh," but lusting implies more than a simple desire. When we are thirsty, we desire a drink of water. That is not lustful. Lusting implies an inordinate or inappropriate desire. *Lust of the flesh* implies an inappropriate desire to satisfy our natural body, that is, while we are living in this flesh. It could be lusting after inappropriate sexual gratification. It could be overindulging in eating or drinking alcohol or in some other substance abuse, or an addiction to some form of entertainment. The natural cravings of our human nature, if not mastered, will soon master us, and they may do it almost imperceptibly. Such lusts and their temporary fulfillment will soon plunge one into further evil. They cause the drug addict to steal, injure or kill. Likewise, the addicted gambler may soon find himself heavily indebted, causing him to take foolish actions with his family's possessions and very well-being. One man I read about made only one mistake in his marital faithfulness and ended up with AIDS and a wife who died as a result, leaving small children motherless. Finally, he died from the disease. That is an example of *the lust of the flesh*, regardless of the immediacy of the effects. It is said to be *of the world*. It can lead a person to abandon his or her walk with God.

> *Galatians 5:16-17 (NKJV)*
> *[16] I say then: Walk in the Spirit, and you shall not fulfill the lust of the flesh. [17] For the flesh lusts against the Spirit, and the Spirit against the flesh; and these are contrary to one another, so that you do not do the things that you wish.*

The remedy to living in the way of the world is to *Walk in the Spirit*. When the mind and the heart are committed to God through Jesus the Son, the Holy Spirit works in that mind and heart. The result is a heart that desires to please God. Being obedient is no longer contrary to the heart, but consistent with it.

> *2 Corinthians 5:17 (NIV2011)*
> *[17] Therefore, if anyone is in Christ, the new creation has come: The old has gone, the new is here!*

> *Galatians 6:14 (ESV)*
> *[14] But far be it from me to boast except in the cross of our Lord*

Jesus Christ, by which the world has been crucified to me, and I to the world.

Perhaps the ultimate example of the *lust of the flesh* found in scripture is Esau, the twin brother of Jacob. Esau was the firstborn and so would have been the traditional recipient of the birthright of his father's inheritance. In his case, that meant much more than just a double portion of the material wealth. It meant he would be the third-generation patriarch of God's redemptive agenda, realized in the messianic lineage of promise. About him we read:

> *Genesis 25:29-34 (NKJV)*
> *[29] Now Jacob cooked a stew; and Esau came in from the field, and he was weary. [30] And Esau said to Jacob, "Please feed me with that same red stew, for I am weary." Therefore his name was called Edom. [31] But Jacob said, "Sell me your birthright as of this day." [32] And Esau said, "Look, I am about to die; so what is this birthright to me?" [33] Then Jacob said, "Swear to me as of this day." So he swore to him, and sold his birthright to Jacob. [34] And Jacob gave Esau bread and stew of lentils; then he ate and drank, arose, and went his way. Thus Esau despised his birthright.*

That choice haunted Esau the rest of his life and made him infamous. The writer of Hebrews used him as a bad example nearly 2000 years later.

> *Hebrews 12:15-17 (NKJV)*
> *...[15] looking carefully lest anyone fall short of the grace of God; lest any root of bitterness springing up cause trouble, and by this many become defiled; [16] lest there be any fornicator or profane person like Esau, who for one morsel of food sold his birthright. [17] For you know that afterward, when he wanted to inherit the blessing, he was rejected, for he found no place for repentance, though he sought it diligently with tears.*

The Lust of the Eyes

The lust of the eyes describes the human craving to attain or possess earthly things. Ownership itself is not the problem. The issue is that, like with so many other areas of life, the good things the Lord allows us to enjoy can become corrupted in our hearts. We begin to put more importance on those gifts than on the One who gave them to us. Two of the ten commandments, eight and ten, address issues related to the lust of the eyes:

> *Exodus 20:15-17 (NKJV)*
> [15] *"You shall not steal . . .* [17] *"You shall not covet your neighbor's house; you shall not covet your neighbor's wife, nor his male servant, nor his female servant, nor his ox, nor his donkey, nor anything that is your neighbor's."*

> *Deuteronomy 8:17-20 (NKJV)*
> [17] *then you say in your heart, 'My power and the might of my hand have gained me this wealth.'* [18] *And you shall remember the LORD your God, for it is He who gives you power to get wealth, that He may establish His covenant which He swore to your fathers, as it is this day.* [19] *Then it shall be, if you by any means forget the LORD your God, and follow other gods, and serve them and worship them, I testify against you this day that you shall surely perish.* [20] *As the nations which the LORD destroys before you, so you shall perish, because you would not be obedient to the voice of the LORD your God.*

Jesus himself taught the people of Galilee to invest their treasure in heaven rather than among men, with the eternal rather than the temporary, in a secure place instead of a place beset with loss.

> *Matthew 6:19-21 (NKJV)*
> [19] *"Do not lay up for yourselves treasures on earth, where moth and rust destroy and where thieves break in and steal;* [20] *but lay up for yourselves treasures in heaven, where neither moth nor rust destroys and where thieves do not break in and steal.* [21] *For where your treasure is, there your heart will be also.*

> *Matthew 6:31-33 (NKJV)*
> [31] *Therefore do not worry, saying, 'What shall we eat?' or 'What shall we drink?' or 'What shall we wear?'* [32] *For after all these things the Gentiles seek. For your heavenly Father knows that you need all these things.* [33] *But seek first the kingdom of God and His righteousness, and all these things shall be added to you.*

The danger of seeking riches is much greater than just losing our investment in this life, or simply having too many possessions. Scripture speaks repeatedly about wealth, and much of it is warnings about the corrupting potential of making the accumulation of material wealth your objective. The lust for riches contaminates the heart. It can reshape one's whole being into an addiction (or worship) of *created things rather than the Creator*. It can lower our life goals to being defined by measureable things rather than by character. It causes us to lose a keen view of God.

Ecclesiastes 5:10-13 (NKJV)
[10] He who loves silver will not be satisfied with silver; Nor he who loves abundance, with increase. This also is vanity. [11] When goods increase, They increase who eat them; So what profit have the owners Except to see them with their eyes? [12] The sleep of a laboring man is sweet, Whether he eats little or much; But the abundance of the rich will not permit him to sleep. [13] There is a severe evil which I have seen under the sun: Riches kept for their owner to his hurt.

Proverbs 15:27 (NKJV)
[27] He who is greedy for gain troubles his own house, But he who hates bribes will live.

Luke 12:13-21 (ESV)
[13] Someone in the crowd said to him, "Teacher, tell my brother to divide the inheritance with me." [14] But he said to him, "Man, who made me a judge or arbitrator over you?" [15] And he said to them, "Take care, and be on your guard against all covetousness, for one's life does not consist in the abundance of his possessions." [16] And he told them a parable, saying, "The land of a rich man produced plentifully, [17] and he thought to himself, 'What shall I do, for I have nowhere to store my crops?' [18] And he said, 'I will do this: I will tear down my barns and build larger ones, and there I will store all my grain and my goods. [19] And I will say to my soul, Soul, you have ample goods laid up for many years; relax, eat, drink, be merry.' [20] But God said to him, 'Fool! This night your soul is required of you, and the things you have prepared, whose will they be?' [21] So is the one who lays up treasure for himself and is not rich toward God."

> *1 Timothy 6:9-10 (NKJV)*
> *⁹ But those who desire to be rich fall into temptation and a snare, and into many foolish and harmful lusts which drown men in destruction and perdition. ¹⁰ For the love of money is a root of all kinds of evil, for which some have strayed from the faith in their greediness, and pierced themselves through with many sorrows.*

Judas Iscariot was one of the twelve apostles, yet was motivated by greed during his latter tenure with Jesus. He was vulnerable to the *lust of the eye*s, as indicated by John's narrative account of Mary, sister of Lazarus, anointing Jesus' feet with costly perfume.

> *John 12:1-6 (NKJV)*
> *¹ Then, six days before the Passover, Jesus came to Bethany, where Lazarus was who had been dead, whom He had raised from the dead. ² There they made Him a supper; and Martha served, but Lazarus was one of those who sat at the table with Him. ³ Then Mary took a pound of very costly oil of spikenard, anointed the feet of Jesus, and wiped His feet with her hair. And the house was filled with the fragrance of the oil. ⁴ Then one of His disciples, Judas Iscariot, Simon's son, who would betray Him, said, ⁵ "Why was this fragrant oil not sold for three hundred denarii and given to the poor?" ⁶ This he said, not that he cared for the poor, but because he was a thief, and had the money box; and he used to take what was put in it.*

Judas was consumed by greed to the extent that he ultimately betrayed Jesus into the hands of the high priests for money.

> *Matthew 26:15 (NKJV)*
> *¹⁵ and said, "What are you willing to give me if I deliver Him to you?" And they counted out to him thirty pieces of silver.*

Contrast Judas with Matthew, another of the twelve who was previously a hated tax collector. While Judas grew more greedy, Matthew, after an encounter with Jesus, left his tax collecting tables behind and followed Jesus, growing in the grace of God. He wrote what has become the first book of the New Testament. God calls us to turn away from the motivations of the world, to throw them off, and to seek after Him.

Material wealth can endanger one whose heart is not rich toward God. It can become an idol because it keeps him focused on a false life-goal, a false god. For some, the issue is the possessiveness of wealth or material possessions (stingy, hoarding). For others, it is the accumulating process of those possessions that is addictive and insatiable (greed). For many, it is the envy of others who have more than you do (jealousy). *The lust of the eyes* is often coupled with the other two areas of temptation, (*lust of the flesh* and *pride of life*) as in the case of the rich man who was not rich toward God, being predisposed to personal ease and carelessness.

The Pride of Life

The *pride of life* is a category of motivation and temptation that deals with the human ego. All of us are vulnerable to it in some form. In our Jeremiah theme passage, it shows up as self-pride because of one's wisdom, or perceived wisdom. This is also how it was unveiled in the original temptation of Eve in Eden. She saw that the forbidden fruit *was desirable to make one wise.*

At this point, it is needful that we consider what is meant by wisdom. Wisdom is viewed as a virtue in many places in scripture. The pursuit of it is a worthy endeavor, especially in the Old Testament book of Proverbs. So—is wisdom a virtue to our faith or a hindrance?

What is wisdom? It is not equivalent to knowledge; there is a difference between wisdom and knowledge. In a nutshell, wisdom is the skill of appropriately and effectively applying knowledge to achieve a practical result. It is like the skill of an accomplished artist who puts his understanding of color theory and perspective down on canvas. It is like the engineer who utilizes scientific principles to create a practical design for a bridge.

We have all experienced people who are full of knowledge, or sometimes trivia, but seem to lack common sense. They may fancy themselves good conversationalists and so spout their knowledge relentlessly. They lack wisdom, not realizing that they are distancing themselves from those around them who see them as pompous.

> *James 4:16 (ESV)*
> *[16] As it is, you boast in your arrogance. All such boasting is evil.*

What is wisdom from a biblical perspective? Not only is there a distinction between knowledge and wisdom, but both Old and New Testaments clearly present two different concepts of wisdom. There is worldly (natural, human) wisdom and there is the wisdom of God. Human wisdom is a gift from God, bestowed when He created us *in His own image*. However, since our fall, that wisdom no longer tracks with God, no longer follows the original pattern, and falls short of that image.

> *Isaiah 55:8-9 (NKJV)*
> *[8] "For My thoughts are not your thoughts, Nor are your ways My ways," says the LORD. [9] "For as the heavens are higher than the earth, So are My ways higher than your ways, And My thoughts than your thoughts.*

> *1 Corinthians 3:18-21 (NKJV)*
> *[18] Let no one deceive himself. If anyone among you seems to be wise in this age, let him become a fool that he may become wise. [19] For the wisdom of this world is foolishness with God. For it is written, "He catches the wise in their own craftiness"; [20] and again, "The LORD knows the thoughts of the wise, that they are futile." [21] Therefore let no one boast in men. For all things are yours:*

> *Romans 1:18-22 (NKJV)*
> *[18] For the wrath of God is revealed from heaven against all ungodliness and unrighteousness of men, who suppress the truth in unrighteousness, [19] because what may be known of God is manifest in them, for God has shown it to them. [20] For since the creation of the world His invisible attributes are clearly seen, being understood by the things that are made, even His eternal power and Godhead, so that they are without excuse, [21] because, although they knew God, they did not glorify Him as God, nor were thankful, but became futile in their thoughts, and their foolish hearts were darkened. [22] Professing to be wise, they became fools, . . .*

Natural wisdom is not evil, in itself. We all learn knowledge and practical wisdom from many sources. We utilize it regularly. When I am getting ready to have major surgery, I am less concerned about the spiritual condition of the surgeon and more interested in his skill and experience as a surgeon. However, true wisdom learns to discern and filter ideas that are inconsistent with the perfect wisdom of God. This presumes a knowledge of that divine wisdom. Thus, Solomon wrote:

Proverbs 9:10 (NKJV)
¹⁰ "The fear of the LORD is the beginning of wisdom, And the knowledge of the Holy One is understanding.

When we recognize in humility that our wisdom falls far short of God's, and choose to seek after Him on His terms, that decision positions us to receive the leading of God's Holy Spirit. He leads us into true wisdom:

John 14:16-18 (NKJV)
¹⁶ And I will pray the Father, and He will give you another Helper, that He may abide with you forever—¹⁷ the Spirit of truth, whom the world cannot receive, because it neither sees Him nor knows Him; but you know Him, for He dwells with you and will be in you. ¹⁸ I will not leave you orphans; I will come to you.

John 7:38-39 (NKJV)
³⁸ He who believes in Me, as the Scripture has said, out of his heart will flow rivers of living water." ³⁹ But this He spoke concerning the Spirit, whom those believing in Him would receive; for the Holy Spirit was not yet given, because Jesus was not yet glorified.

1 Corinthians 2:9-10 (NKJV)
⁹ But as it is written: "Eye has not seen, nor ear heard, Nor have entered into the heart of man The things which God has prepared for those who love Him." ¹⁰ But God has revealed them to us through His Spirit. For the Spirit searches all things, yes, the deep things of God.

The things of God cannot be perceived by our natural senses or imagined by the natural heart. They are perceived by revelation that comes from the Holy Spirit working within us.

Natural wisdom can masquerade as religious truth. False doctrines can deceive one so that he cannot distinguish poor theology from true theology.

> *Matthew 7:21-23 (NKJV)*
> [21] *"Not everyone who says to Me, 'Lord, Lord,' shall enter the kingdom of heaven, but he who does the will of My Father in heaven.* [22] *Many will say to Me in that day, 'Lord, Lord, have we not prophesied in Your name, cast out demons in Your name, and done many wonders in Your name?'* [23] *And then I will declare to them, 'I never knew you; depart from Me, you who practice lawlessness!'*

> *Philippians 3:3-11 (NKJV)*
> [3] *For we are the circumcision, who worship God in the Spirit, rejoice in Christ Jesus, and have no confidence in the flesh,* [4] *though I also might have confidence in the flesh. If anyone else thinks he may have confidence in the flesh, I more so:* [5] *circumcised the eighth day, of the stock of Israel, of the tribe of Benjamin, a Hebrew of the Hebrews; concerning the law, a Pharisee;* [6] *concerning zeal, persecuting the church; concerning the righteousness which is in the law, blameless.* [7] *But what things were gain to me, these I have counted loss for Christ.* [8] *Yet indeed I also count all things loss for the excellence of the knowledge of Christ Jesus my Lord, for whom I have suffered the loss of all things, and count them as rubbish, that I may gain Christ* [9] *and be found in Him, not having my own righteousness, which is from the law, but that which is through faith in Christ, the righteousness which is from God by faith;* [10] *that I may know Him and the power of His resurrection, and the fellowship of His sufferings, being conformed to His death,* [11] *if, by any means, I may attain to the resurrection from the dead.*

> *Galatians 6:12-14 (NKJV)*
> [12] *As many as desire to make a good showing in the flesh, these would compel you to be circumcised, only that they may not*

suffer persecution for the cross of Christ. [13] *For not even those who are circumcised keep the law, but they desire to have you circumcised that they may boast in your flesh.* [14] *But God forbid that I should boast except in the cross of our Lord Jesus Christ, by whom the world has been crucified to me, and I to the world.*

All 'wisdom' should be scrutinized as to whether or not it is consistent with biblical truth. We Christians are not called to categorically discard every statement made by the world, but we must filter all incoming information. How do we know if it is consistent? The only way is to learn biblical truth for ourselves. Storing up scripture in our memory is our preparation for discerning falsehood.

Psalm 119:9-11 (NKJV)
[9] *How can a young man cleanse his way? By taking heed according to Your word.* [10] *With my whole heart I have sought You; Oh, let me not wander from Your commandments!* [11] *Your word I have hidden in my heart, That I might not sin against You!*

The world has all kinds of 'wisdom' to tell us. This necessity to filter out bad wisdom is not an occasional thing. Incoming worldly wisdom is a constant barrage. Our filter must also be alert and functional. Wisdom comes at us from special interests trying to sell a product. It comes from social agendas trying to make their case. It comes in the media. It comes in false religion. It comes in subtle poignant movie moments such as when Ali McGraw told Ryan O'Neal in the film Love Story, "Love means never having to say you're sorry." Today, there are a lot of people who bought into that lie. They will not accept any responsibility in a relationship rift. They cannot say, "I'm sorry." It begins with, "I will not" but soon becomes, "I cannot" as they train themselves in the ways of self-pride. It is obvious they lacked the basis to filter out bad advice.

Specific Applications of Things to Not Boast About
Within the three realms of motivation we have been discussing, there are a number of specific applications highlighted in scripture that bear knowing and taking heed. First, is the error of presumption. This happens when we think we direct our own destiny, removing God from atop our motivation hierarchy.

Proverbs 27:1 (ESV)
¹ Do not boast about tomorrow, for you do not know what a day may bring.

Presumption is an insult to God, assuming we control our own destiny instead of fearing Him who holds our future in His hands. The man or woman of presumption says:

Isaiah 56:12 (NIV2011)
¹² "Come," each one cries, "let me get wine! Let us drink our fill of beer! And tomorrow will be like today, or even far better."

Luke 12:19-20 (NIV2011)
¹⁹ And I'll say to myself, "You have plenty of grain laid up for many years. Take life easy; eat, drink and be merry." ' ²⁰ "But God said to him, 'You fool! This very night your life will be demanded from you. Then who will get what you have prepared for yourself?'

James 4:13-16 (NIV2011)
¹³ Now listen, you who say, "Today or tomorrow we will go to this or that city, spend a year there, carry on business and make money." ¹⁴ Why, you do not even know what will happen tomorrow. What is your life? You are a mist that appears for a little while and then vanishes. ¹⁵ Instead, you ought to say, "If it is the Lord's will, we will live and do this or that." ¹⁶ As it is, you boast in your arrogant schemes. All such boasting is evil.

Second is this matter of boasting about one's self. This takes various forms. Everyone battles with issues of the ego. For some, this shows itself in self-aggrandizement. Solomon advises us otherwise.

Proverbs 27:2-3 (ESV)
² Let another praise you, and not your own mouth; a stranger, and not your own lips. ³ A stone is heavy, and sand is weighty, but a fool's provocation is heavier than both.

And the psalmist equates boasting with the wicked.

Psalm 94:3-4 (ESV)
³ O LORD, how long shall the wicked, how long shall the

wicked exult? *⁴ They pour out their arrogant words; all the evildoers boast.*

Paul, in the New Testament, differentiates between confidence on the one hand with arrogant boasting on the other. He defends his boldness as being confidence in the Lord, not in himself.

> *2 Corinthians 10:8-18 (ESV)*
> *⁸ For even if I boast a little too much of our authority, which the Lord gave for building you up and not for destroying you, I will not be ashamed. ⁹ I do not want to appear to be frightening you with my letters. ¹⁰ For they* [Paul's critics] *say, "His letters are weighty and strong, but his bodily presence is weak, and his speech of no account." ¹¹ Let such a person understand that what we say by letter when absent, we do when present. ¹² Not that we dare to classify or compare ourselves with some of those who are commending themselves. But when they measure themselves by one another and compare themselves with one another, they are without understanding. ¹³ But we will not boast beyond limits, but will boast only with regard to the area of influence God assigned to us, to reach even to you. ¹⁴ For we are not overextending ourselves, as though we did not reach you. For we were the first to come all the way to you with the gospel of Christ. ¹⁵ We do not boast beyond limit in the labors of others. But our hope is that as your faith increases, our area of influence among you may be greatly enlarged, ¹⁶ so that we may preach the gospel in lands beyond you, without boasting of work already done in another's area of influence. ¹⁷ "Let the one who boasts, boast in the Lord." ¹⁸ For it is not the one who commends himself who is approved, but the one whom the Lord commends.*

He is not commending himself except to show the authority given him by the Lord. Note that he quotes from our theme passage. Paul is looking for the commendation that comes from God.

Another evidence of ego problems is despising authority. Authority is instituted by God for the maintaining of a relatively peaceful life.

> *2 Peter 2:10 (NKJV)*
> *¹⁰ and especially those who walk according to the flesh in the*

lust of uncleanness and despise authority. They are presumptuous, self-willed. They are not afraid to speak evil of dignitaries,

Not all in authority personally deserve honor and praise, but their position of authority calls for submission and respect. God is the one who instituted authority and submission for the civil peacefulness of men. Christians are specifically instructed in scripture to show proper regard and obedience to such authority on that basis alone. Jesus taught us:

> Mark 12:15-17 (NKJV)
> [15] *Shall we pay, or shall we not pay?" But He, knowing their hypocrisy, said to them, "Why do you test Me? Bring Me a denarius that I may see it."* [16] *So they brought it. And He said to them, "Whose image and inscription is this?" They said to Him, "Caesar's."* [17] *And Jesus answered and said to them, "Render to Caesar the things that are Caesar's, and to God the things that are God's." And they marveled at Him.*

And both Paul and Peter taught:

> Romans 13:1-2 (NKJV)
> [1] *Let every soul be subject to the governing authorities. For there is no authority except from God, and the authorities that exist are appointed by God.* [2] *Therefore whoever resists the authority resists the ordinance of God, and those who resist will bring judgment on themselves.*

> 1 Peter 2:13-15 (NKJV)
> [13] *Therefore submit yourselves to every ordinance of man for the Lord's sake, whether to the king as supreme,* [14] *or to governors, as to those who are sent by him for the punishment of evildoers and for the praise of those who do good.* [15] *For this is the will of God, that by doing good you may put to silence the ignorance of foolish men-*

To exult oneself over governing authorities gives evidence to a lack of humility. A person can be doctrinally or politically correct, yet be dead wrong in his overarching persona by speaking disrespectfully of God's ordained leaders. This principle is seen in David in the Old

Testament when he refused to speak against or lift up his hand against King Saul, *the Lord's anointed*, even though Saul had tried to kill him several times out of envy.

This willing submission applies to all instituted venues of authority such as civil government, the church, the family and an employer. Yes, there are boundaries for authority in each of these areas and we could expound on this topic, but won't because we don't want to stray from our main theme. Lack of respect and obedience to authority is often a sign of excessive pride and is a form of arrogant boasting.

To summarize, let us understand the three areas of temptation for fulfillment in this life. These are the *lust of the flesh*, the *lust of the eyes* and the *pride of life*. There is a pride element associated with each of these areas, causing us to boast about our involvement in them.

May we learn of the Lord through His written word so that we are equipped to discern error from truth, evil from good, false motives from pure motives. We must train ourselves in this wisdom. It does not come naturally. We train through purposeful, diligent study of the Bible. May we, over our lifetime, grow in that kind of wisdom that begins with *the fear of the Lord*.

Chapter 4
SOMETHING TO BOAST ABOUT

Jeremiah 9:23-24 (ESV)
[23] Thus says the LORD: "Let not the wise man boast in his wisdom, let not the mighty man boast in his might, let not the rich man boast in his riches, [24] but let him who boasts boast in this, that he understands and knows me, that I am the LORD who practices steadfast love, justice, and righteousness in the earth. For in these things I delight, declares the LORD."

Our theme passage prohibits boasting about many things, but it says there is one thing that is worthy to boast about. If a person *understands and knows* God, that is worthy of boasting. In this one verse of scripture, God gives us a priority list. Knowing God should be our greatest quest. It should set our priorities for life. It should govern our behavior. In short, if we have a genuinely divine perspective, the thirst for a knowledge of God should consume our thoughts and determine our preferences. If we could conceive the worth of intimately knowing God, that is, to comprehend how indescribably valuable God Himself is to us, we would direct everything we do and say and think toward that end. Jesus taught us this priority clearly in two short parables.

Matthew 13:44-46 (NIV2011)
[44] "The kingdom of heaven is like treasure hidden in a field. When a man found it, he hid it again, and then in his joy went and sold all he had and bought that field. [45] "Again, the kingdom of heaven is like a merchant looking for fine pearls. [46] When he found one of great value, he went away and sold everything he had and bought it.

In each of these parables there are two questions that the hearer is compelled to confront. The first one is implicitly asked and explicitly addressed in each case. It is, "How much did it cost the finder?" In both parables, the answer is clearly given: *all he had*. The second question that more subtly thrusts itself into our mind is, "Was it worth the price?" The second question and its answer is implied in both parables. In fact, this implied question and answer are the main point of each parable. In each parable, the answer to the second question is clearly "yes; it was well worth the price," without reservation. Both the field worker and the pearl merchant were filled with joy at their discovery. The worth of their found treasure was so obvious that they moved decisively, without deliberation, to acquire it. It was the buy of a lifetime.

These two short parables vividly portray the surpassing value of the kingdom of heaven in a person's life. The abiding sovereignty of Christ as Lord really cannot be weighed on any temporal scale. It is the source of worthwhile purpose. It is the source of joy, even in the midst of struggles. It is the source of love, the unconditional kind that comes from God. It is the source of peace, peace of soul. It is the source of hope, and herein is its greatest value. Its value is eternal. Nothing else offers and delivers all of this.

<u>Knowing God, Loving God</u>
Acquiring the kingdom of heaven is that kind of treasure. What do phrases like *the kingdom of God, salvation* and *eternal life* have to do with knowing God? The answer is 'everything.' Knowing God is both the means and the reward of entering eternal life in heaven. Heaven is not just a place. It is much more. Jesus said it in his prayer, just before his arrest and execution.

> *John 17:3 (NIV2011)*
> *3 Now this is eternal life: that they know you, the only true God, and Jesus Christ, whom you have sent.*

And in his sermon on the mount, he taught this negative truth:

> *Matthew 7:22-23 (NIV2011)*
> *[22] Many will say to me on that day, Lord, Lord, did we not prophesy in your name and in your name drive out demons and in your name perform many miracles [23] Then I will tell them plainly, I never knew you. Away from me, you evildoers!*

Now, this kind of knowing we are speaking of goes beyond intellectual familiarity with someone. It develops into affection, into friendship, perhaps into some level of intimacy, and eventually into love. Love is the ultimate objective of the knowing process.

In eternity, our relationship with God will be our consummate reward. Knowing God is to have a relationship with Him. In this life, it is to have an intimacy through faith in the revealed person of God in Christ Jesus and to cherish that relationship. That is the hidden treasure and the valuable pearl. As we see in scripture God's self-revelation, we begin to comprehend how wonderful He is, how great is His worth and how inestimable the value of His presence. Thus, our relationship with Him becomes not only the way to acquire eternal life, but also the very essence of our reward. God's intimate friendship is our all-sufficient reward. Paul extolled the value of owning the good news from his own experience with Jesus:

> *Philippians 3:3-11 (NIV2011)*
> *³ For it is we who are the circumcision, we who serve God by his Spirit, who boast in Christ Jesus, and who put no confidence in the flesh, ⁴ though I myself have reasons for such confidence. If someone else thinks they have reasons to put confidence in the flesh, I have more: ⁵ circumcised on the eighth day, of the people of Israel, of the tribe of Benjamin, a Hebrew of Hebrews; in regard to the law, a Pharisee; ⁶ as for zeal, persecuting the church; as for righteousness based on the law, faultless. ⁷ But whatever were gains to me I now consider loss for the sake of Christ. ⁸ What is more, I consider everything a loss because of the surpassing worth of knowing Christ Jesus my Lord, for whose sake I have lost all things. I consider them garbage, that I may gain Christ ⁹ and be found in him, not having a righteousness of my own that comes from the law, but that which is through faith in Christ, the righteousness that comes from God on the basis of faith. ¹⁰ I want to know Christ, yes, to know the power of his resurrection and participation in his sufferings, becoming like him in his death, ¹¹ and so, somehow, attaining to the resurrection from the dead.*

The Old Testament summarizes the commandments of God into two overarching principles:

> *Deuteronomy 6:4-5 (NIV2011)*
> *⁴ Hear, O Israel: The LORD our God, the LORD is one. ⁵ Love the LORD your God with all your heart and with all your soul and with all your strength.*

> *Leviticus 19:18 (NIV2011)*
> *[18] Do not seek revenge or bear a grudge against anyone among your people, but love your neighbor as yourself. I am the LORD.*

Jesus combined and quoted these two passage in his teaching:

> *Luke 10:25-27 (NIV2011)*
> *[25] On one occasion an expert in the law stood up to test Jesus. Teacher, he asked, what must I do to inherit eternal life? [26] What is written in the Law? he replied. How do you read it? [27] He answered, Love the Lord your God with all your heart and with all your soul and with all your strength and with all your mind; and, Love your neighbor as yourself. [28] You have answered correctly, Jesus replied. Do this and you will live.*

The second principle or command was not a command to love our neighbors because they are loveable, or because it makes for a more orderly civic lifestyle. It is a command to love them because they are made in the image of God.

> *1 John 4:20 (NKJV)*
> *[20] If someone says, "I love God," and hates his brother, he is a liar; for he who does not love his brother whom he has seen, how can he love God whom he has not seen?*

> *Genesis 1:26-27 (NIV2011)*
> *[26] Then God said, "Let us make mankind in our image, in our likeness, so that they may rule over the fish in the sea and the birds in the sky, over the livestock and all the wild animals, and over all the creatures that move along the ground." [27] So God created mankind in his own image, in the image of God he created them; male and female he created them.*

Thus, both commands point to the worthiness of God to be loved. We do not naturally love those we do not know. Therefore, knowing God is the foundation for our relationship with Him. So close is that relationship that scripture compares it to being fellow-citizens, even further as being of the same family with God.

> *Ephesians 2:19 (NIV2011)*
> *[19] Consequently, you are no longer foreigners and strangers,*

> but fellow citizens with God's people and also members of his household,

> 1 John 5:19 (NIV2011)
> ¹⁹ We know that we are children of God . . .

As if that were not intense enough, God further compares us to being a bride, and Jesus as the bridegroom. The intimacy of romantic love is thus used metaphorically to describe the intensity of love in our relationship with God.

> Ephesians 5:31-32 (NIV2011)
> ³¹ "For this reason a man will leave his father and mother and be united to his wife, and the two will become one flesh." ³² This is a profound mystery—but I am talking about Christ and the church.

> Revelation 19:6-9 (NKJV)
> ⁶ And I heard, as it were, the voice of a great multitude, as the sound of many waters and as the sound of mighty thunderings, saying, "Alleluia! For the Lord God Omnipotent reigns! ⁷ Let us be glad and rejoice and give Him glory, for the marriage of the Lamb has come, and His wife has made herself ready."
> ⁸ And to her it was granted to be arrayed in fine linen, clean and bright, for the fine linen is the righteous acts of the saints.
> ⁹ Then he said to me, "Write: 'Blessed are those who are called to the marriage supper of the Lamb!' " And he said to me, "These are the true sayings of God."

Thus, we see from scripture that God desires a relationship with you. For your part, it begins with learning who God is, what He is like, and what He is not. These are learned from study of scripture. The Bible is God's love-letter to you. It is His resume. With the guiding of God's Spirit, this newfound knowledge soon makes Jesus seem like a friend, not just an interesting historical figure. Finally comes a devoted commitment to love Him like a bride loves her husband. This kind of knowing is what Jesus had in mind when he stated, *Now this is eternal life, that they may know you, the only true God, and Jesus Christ whom you have sent.*

Revealed Truth
This intimate knowledge doesn't just occur by itself. Since we can't see God and all His glorious attributes, we would know nothing of Him if He did not make Himself known to us in a way we can comprehend. That is just what He has done. He has revealed Himself in two main ways. First, He has made Himself somewhat known to us in a deductive way through 'general revelation.' This primarily includes observations of the world around us giving evidence of His existence. When we gaze at the vastness of the night sky or at the intricate workings of a single organic cell, elementary intelligence sees in them a Creator. The evidence of God is hundreds of times more evident in our day, with telescopes, electron microscopes and scientific analytical methods, than in the days the scriptures were written. Yet the resistance to God by the secular world is greater than ever. Man's ability to avoid God's obvious truth has risen to the occasion, making him blind to his own ignorance.

Romans 1:20-22 (NKJV)
[20] For since the creation of the world His invisible attributes are clearly seen, being understood by the things that are made, even His eternal power and Godhead, so that they are without excuse, [21] because, although they knew God, they did not glorify Him as God, nor were thankful, but became futile in their thoughts, and their foolish hearts were darkened. [22] Professing to be wise, they became fools,

The reality and nature of God is revealed a second way. This is called 'special revelation.' This type of revelation comes when God breaks into our realm of experience through either providential or miraculous ways to communicate with us. In the past, many of God's self-revelations were revealed to men, which He caused to be written for the comprehension of future generations. Scripture is special revelation. Beyond scripture, God's special revelation can speak to us in various ways such as through the Holy Spirit to our spirit, or through answered prayer. However, only the special revelation of scripture is able to make us *wise unto salvation.*

Both general revelation and special revelation give witness to the existence and enormity of the Creator. In Psalm 19, David incorporates both into his praise of God's greatness. Verses 1-6 speak of His general revelation through the witness of the creation itself.

Special revelation, His written word, is exalted in verses 7-14 in bringing about a knowledge of God.

> *Psalm 19:1-14 (NKJV)*
> *[1] The heavens declare the glory of God; And the firmament shows His handiwork. [2] Day unto day utters speech, And night unto night reveals knowledge. [3] There is no speech nor language where their voice is not heard. [4] Their line has gone out through all the earth, And their words to the end of the world. In them He has set a tabernacle for the sun, [5] which is like a bridegroom coming out of his chamber, And rejoices like a strong man to run its race. [6] Its rising is from one end of heaven, And its circuit to the other end; And there is nothing hidden from its heat. [7] The law of the LORD is perfect, converting the soul; The testimony of the LORD is sure, making wise the simple; [8] The statutes of the LORD are right, rejoicing the heart; The commandment of the LORD is pure, enlightening the eyes; [9] The fear of the LORD is clean, enduring forever; The judgments of the LORD are true and righteous altogether. [10] More to be desired are they than gold, Yea, than much fine gold; Sweeter also than honey and the honeycomb. [11] Moreover by them Your servant is warned, And in keeping them there is great reward. [12] Who can understand his errors? Cleanse me from secret faults. [13] Keep back Your servant also from presumptuous sins; Let them not have dominion over me. Then I shall be blameless, And I shall be innocent of great transgression. [14] Let the words of my mouth and the meditation of my heart Be acceptable in Your sight, O LORD, my strength and my Redeemer.*

At various times in the past, God revealed Himself to certain chosen people: the patriarchs, the judges, the priests and prophets of the Old Testament. He revealed Himself in dreams and visions. He showed Himself indirectly to Moses in glory, as well as in great signs and wonders. He revealed Himself in supernatural military victories for the Israelites. He spoke indirectly through carefully prescribed worship practices and in tabernacle and temple design. He spoke in symbolic historical events such as the great flood and in the original Passover. He revealed Himself through providential oversight of His chosen people, as revealed in the events of Ezra, Nehemiah and Esther. He spoke through His prophets, giving the validating evidence of fulfillment. Then, as the writer of Hebrews tells us . . .

> *Hebrews 1:1-3 (NKJV)*
> *¹ God, who at various times and in various ways spoke in time past to the fathers by the prophets, ² has in these last days spoken to us by His Son, whom He has appointed heir of all things, through whom also He made the worlds; ³ who being the brightness of His glory and the express image of His person, and upholding all things by the word of His power, when He had by Himself purged our sins, sat down at the right hand of the Majesty on high,*

Jesus is the ultimate revelation by God of Himself to man. Jesus revealed God in his incarnation, in his resurrection, and in his glory. This self-revelation of Himself in the human context, along with its direct relevance and application to our eternal future, is the gospel.

Of course, all of these revelations of God would be lost to us, if not for the fact that He caused them to be written down for future generations. The Bible is the record of that revelation. They are not messages by man about God, but messages from God, through men, about God.

> *Deuteronomy 29:29 (NIV2011)*
> *²⁹ The secret things belong to the LORD our God, but the things revealed belong to us and to our children forever, that we may follow all the words of this law.*

> *2 Peter 1:20-21 (NIV2011)*
> *²⁰ Above all, you must understand that no prophecy of Scripture came about by the prophet's own interpretation of things. ²¹ For prophecy never had its origin in the human will, but prophets, though human, spoke from God as they were carried along by the Holy Spirit.*

> *1 Peter 1:23 (NIV2011)*
> *²³ For you have been born again, not of perishable seed, but of imperishable, through the living and enduring word of God.*

> *1 Thessalonians 2:13 (NIV2011)*
> *¹³ And we also thank God continually because, when you received the word of God, which you heard from us, you*

accepted it not as a human word, but as it actually is, the word of God, which is indeed at work in you who believe.

The recorded special revelation of scripture is more than just words on a page. We tend to assign more validity to words that are printed or written, than to those of casual verbal conversation. There is something about written words that conveys more thoughtfulness, more intentionality, more authority. But scripture is more than just words on a page.

We might be more strongly persuaded to trust the written words when we understand that those words are true and accurate in all that they profess. Scripture claims of itself that it is truth. Jesus told his audience on the hillside of Galilee:

Matthew 5:17-18 (ESV)
[17] *"Do not think that I have come to abolish the Law or the Prophets; I have not come to abolish them but to fulfill them.* [18] *For truly, I say to you, until heaven and earth pass away, not an iota, not a dot, will pass from the Law until all is accomplished.*

Still greater esteem might be given to scripture because it is the very oracles of God, and rightly so. It is the communication of God to us. An autograph or personal note from a famous person is often a valued item. If someone were to meet the president of the United States eye-to-eye, that would be a big deal. The average person would not expect to have such a chance during their lifetime. But to have significant conversation from the Creator of the universe places scripture in a category all by itself because God is in a category all by Himself.

And yet scripture's power is even greater still. It has something no other piece of literature possesses. It has the active power of God behind it. God's written word is effective. Its effectiveness is executed through the work of His Spirit.

Isaiah 55:10-11 (NIV2011)
[10] *As the rain and the snow come down from heaven, and do not return to it without watering the earth and making it bud and flourish, so that it yields seed for the sower and bread for the eater,* [11] *so is my word that goes out from my mouth: It will not*

return to me empty, but will accomplish what I desire and achieve the purpose for which I sent it.

Hebrews 4:12 (NIV2011)
¹² For the word of God is alive and active. Sharper than any double-edged sword, it penetrates even to dividing soul and spirit, joints and marrow; it judges the thoughts and attitudes of the heart.

God is inviting people to Himself. He created us for the very purpose of having a relationship with us, an intimate love relationship. That bond will be an eternal bond, but it begins when we put our trust in Jesus as Lord and Savior.

God is a revealing God because He is a relational God. In His written word, He is first and foremost showing us about Himself. That is our most fundamental need—to know God, the accurate truth about Him, and to be in personal relationship with Him. This is the essence of salvation. The truth about God and the particular manifestation of that truth in the incarnation of Jesus with his atoning sacrificial death and resurrection—this is the message of the *gospel*. It is the good news. It is God's ultimate expression of His love for us.

The apostles, following their Lord's instructions, were fixed on imparting this knowledge of God in Christ Jesus to the early church, written beforehand in scripture and visibly revealed in Jesus. In the following passages, note that in each one, the revealing and reception of this knowledge is discussed at the beginning of their respective letters (in the first chapter of our books of the New Testament.). It is so fundamental to the faith that each writer uses it to lay the opening foundation for his message. The importance of revealed knowledge of God in Jesus shows up again and again in Paul's writings.

Romans 1:1-4 (ESV)
¹ Paul, a servant of Christ Jesus, called to be an apostle, set apart for the gospel of God, ² which he promised beforehand through his prophets in the holy Scriptures, ³ concerning his Son, who was descended from David according to the flesh ⁴ and was declared to be the Son of God in power according to the Spirit of holiness by his resurrection from the dead, Jesus Christ our Lord,

1 Corinthians 1:4-7 (ESV)
⁴ I give thanks to my God always for you because of the grace of God that was given you in Christ Jesus, ⁵ that in every way you were enriched in him in all speech and all knowledge" ⁶ even as the testimony about Christ was confirmed among you" ⁷ so that you are not lacking in any gift, as you wait for the revealing of our Lord Jesus Christ,

Ephesians 1:15-19 (ESV)
¹⁵ For this reason, because I have heard of your faith in the Lord Jesus and your love toward all the saints, ¹⁶ I do not cease to give thanks for you, remembering you in my prayers, ¹⁷ that the God of our Lord Jesus Christ, the Father of glory, may give you the Spirit of wisdom and of revelation in the knowledge of him, ¹⁸ having the eyes of your hearts enlightened, that you may know what is the hope to which he has called you, what are the riches of his glorious inheritance in the saints, ¹⁹ and what is the immeasurable greatness of his power toward us who believe, according to the working of his great might

Colossians 1:9-10 (ESV)
⁹ And so, from the day we heard, we have not ceased to pray for you, asking that you may be filled with the knowledge of his will in all spiritual wisdom and understanding, ¹⁰ so as to walk in a manner worthy of the Lord, fully pleasing to him, bearing fruit in every good work and increasing in the knowledge of God.

Titus 1:1-3 (ESV)
¹ Paul, a servant of God and an apostle of Jesus Christ, for the sake of the faith of God's elect and their knowledge of the truth, which accords with godliness, ² in hope of eternal life, which God, who never lies, promised before the ages began ³ and at the proper time manifested in his word through the preaching with which I have been entrusted by the command of God our Savior;

Likewise, Peter spoke of our revealing God who made Himself known to us through the prophets and their fulfillments in the first advent of Christ.

1 Peter 1:10-12 (ESV)
¹⁰ Concerning this salvation, the prophets who prophesied about the grace that was to be yours searched and inquired carefully, ¹¹ inquiring what person or time the Spirit of Christ in them was indicating when he predicted the sufferings of Christ and the subsequent glories. ¹² It was revealed to them that they were serving not themselves but you, in the things that have now been announced to you through those who preached the good news to you by the Holy Spirit sent from heaven, things into which angels long to look.

2 Peter 1:2 (NIV2011)
² Grace and peace be yours in abundance through the knowledge of God and of Jesus our Lord.

And then John opens his first letter with words like *heard* and *seen with our eyes*, and *touched with our hands, manifest,* and *proclaim*— words of revelation which, for the apostles, were irrefutable evidence of its being revealed truth:

1 John 1:1-3 (NIV2011)
¹ That which was from the beginning, which we have heard, which we have seen with our eyes, which we have looked at and our hands have touched—this we proclaim concerning the Word of life. ² The life appeared; we have seen it and testify to it, and we proclaim to you the eternal life, which was with the Father and has appeared to us. ³ We proclaim to you what we have seen and heard, so that you also may have fellowship with us. And our fellowship is with the Father and with his Son, Jesus Christ.

And John opens his gospel account similarly:

John 1:1,14,18 (NIV2011)
¹ In the beginning was the Word, and the Word was with God, and the Word was God. . . ¹⁴ The Word became flesh and made his dwelling among us. We have seen his glory, the glory of the one and only Son, who came from the Father, full of grace and truth. . . . ¹⁸ No one has ever seen God, but the one and only Son, who is himself God and is in closest relationship with the Father, has made him known.

The Word became flesh. Jesus is that *Word*. By using the word *Word* to identify Christ, he is being set forth as the communication, the manifestation, the very revelation of the Father in human flesh. In all of these scriptures, there is a lot of revealing going on here. A lot of manifesting and giving evidence of the nature of God. The fact that this divine knowledge is spoken of near the beginning (first chapter) of each book in so many cases, speaks of the eminence and priority of this theme.

Divine Relationship
In any relationship, there is a progressive transition evolving. The transition is in growing from one level of knowledge to another; from knowing about a person to knowing him or her. As two people spend time together, they become familiar with each other at an increasing level. They learn to know the other person's personality and temperament, their likes and dislikes, their character qualities and their spiritual condition. It moves from familiarity to acquaintance to fellowship to friendship. If another person asks if you know Jane Doe, you might answer, " I know who she is" or "I have met her once or twice" or "Yes, we are friends", depending on the relationship status. So it is with our relationship with God. Of course, He knows us intimately from the beginning, but He starts out as a stranger to us. Through the process of learning about Him, we move up the relationship ladder. This can occur rapidly or more gradually.

> *1 John 5:20 (NIV2011)*
> [20] *We know also that the Son of God has come and has given us understanding, so that we may know him who is true. And we are in him who is true by being in his Son Jesus Christ. He is the true God and eternal life.*

This is not to say that our justification is partial before it is total. From the time salvation comes, justification is total. But salvation's work is not yet finished. It remains for the justified person to live and to grow in Christ, then ultimately to be glorified, becoming Christlike in their nature. Our knowledge of God may indeed be gradual or incremental. But when we reach a level of faith that is accepted by God as genuine and sufficient, and have responded in faith, the believer is fully justified. God knows when our knowledge of Him and our belief in His redemption plan become saving faith.

When Christ returns in glory, we will suddenly know him in his entirety. To use theological terms, that is when our 'sanctification' (striving for holiness) gives way to glorification (attainment of perfect holiness). Until then, our knowledge of him is partial and growing in our mortal minds. We seek it as best we can through study of His scriptures and in prayer and meditation, through the power of the Holy Spirit, but on that day, we will be instantly changed to be like him in perfect harmony.

> *2 Corinthians 3:18 (ESV)*
> *[18] And we all, with unveiled face, beholding the glory of the Lord, are being transformed into the same image from one degree of glory to another. For this comes from the Lord who is the Spirit.*
>
> *Romans 8:30 (ESV)*
> *[30] And those whom he predestined he also called, and those whom he called he also justified, and those whom he justified he also glorified.*
>
> *1 John 3:2 (NIV2011)*
> *[2] Dear friends, now we are children of God, and what we will be has not yet been made known. But we know that when Christ appears, we shall be like him, for we shall see him as he is.*

The purpose of knowing Jesus is to form a relationship with him, the objective being to become like him in his character qualities. It is to become Christ-like. As for this present time, the likeness of him in us is imperfect. Nevertheless, we do know him in part. We don't say, "I know of him" but rather "Yes, I do know him." He is not a stranger or casual acquaintance, if in fact we have believed in him as Lord and Savior. He is a friend, a closer friend than we often realize. He is a friend who loves us dearly.

> *1 John 5:1-5,11-12 (NIV2011)*
> *[1] Everyone who believes that Jesus is the Christ is born of God, and everyone who loves the father loves his child as well. [2] This is how we know that we love the children of God: by loving God and carrying out his commands. [3] In fact, this is love for God: to keep his commands. And his commands are not burdensome,*

⁴ for everyone born of God overcomes the world. This is the victory that has overcome the world, even our faith. ⁵ Who is it that overcomes the world? Only the one who believes that Jesus is the Son of God. . . . ¹¹ And this is the testimony: God has given us eternal life, and this life is in his Son. ¹² Whoever has the Son has life; whoever does not have the Son of God does not have life.

This is the knowledge of him that is worthy to boast about. *Let him who boasts, boast about this, that he understands and knows me . . .* This is indeed something to boast about! It trumps everything else in this life for several reasons. First, it trumps everything else because God transcends everything else. Second, because it is the ultimate truth of all creative and redemptive reality. Third, because its consequences are eternal. We read in Revelation 5 that the only one in heaven or earth worthy to execute final judgment and to usher in eternal redemption is Jesus. Only Jesus and the Father are worthy of all praise and honor on the basis of his sacrificial death and resurrection. Paul expressed this to the Philippians.

Philippians 3:7-11 (ESV)
⁷ But whatever gain I had, I counted as loss for the sake of Christ. ⁸ Indeed, I count everything as loss because of the surpassing worth of knowing Christ Jesus my Lord. For his sake I have suffered the loss of all things and count them as rubbish, in order that I may gain Christ ⁹ and be found in him, not having a righteousness of my own that comes from the law, but that which comes through faith in Christ, the righteousness from God that depends on faith— ¹⁰ that I may know him and the power of his resurrection, and may share his sufferings, becoming like him in his death, ¹¹ that by any means possible I may attain the resurrection from the dead.

Knowing the Father and the Son is indeed something to boast about. Instead of exalting ourselves, we should in all ways exalt the Lord who made us and empowered us. David did that in all his psalms.

Psalm 34:1-3 (ESV)
¹ I will bless the LORD at all times; his praise shall continually be in my mouth. ² My soul makes its boast in the LORD; let the

humble hear and be glad. ³ *Oh, magnify the LORD with me, and let us exalt his name together!*

And later quoting from our theme verse, Paul reiterated that no one is worthy of boasting about themselves:

1 Corinthians 1:30-31 (ESV)
³⁰ And because of him [God] *you are in Christ Jesus, who became to us wisdom from God, righteousness and sanctification and redemption, ³¹ so that, as it is written, "Let the one who boasts, boast in the Lord."*

The second verse of the Christian hymn, 'When I Survey the Wondrous Cross,' expresses this idea clearly.

> Forbid it, Lord, that I should boast,
> Save in the death of Christ my God!
> All the vain things that charm me most,
> I sacrifice them to His blood.

Chapter 5
THE GOD WE BOAST OF

Our theme passage doesn't end with just knowing a god. It makes sure the God we know is the real, only Creator and Redeemer. It makes sure we know rightly about Him.

> *Jeremiah 9:24 (ESV)*
> *[24] but let him who boasts boast in this, that he understands and knows me, that I am the LORD who practices steadfast love, justice, and righteousness in the earth. For in these things I delight, declares the LORD."*

To know and understand Him in His reality is critical. We are boasting about a god of our own making if we do not know Him accurately. In that case, we are boasting in a counterfeit. That is called 'idolatry.' It is common to hear someone say something like, "My God would never do that," or "Where was God when . . .?" We presume to think that God thinks just like us. But God knows all things; He sees the result of every action. He has eternal purposes in mind, while we can hardly see past the present moment.

When we try to recreate Him to suit our wishes, the result is always a much less glorious personification than He really is. It is an affront to His real nature. If we prefer to assume a god that accommodates our present lifestyle rather than the One Who has revealed Himself to us, we deceive ourselves and offend Him.

Our theme passage makes sure we know some basic truths about God. These may not always be apparent to us while we are entangled in the circumstances of life. Therefore, in His written word, He assures us of His essential nature, His character. If we believe otherwise about Him, we are guilty of sculpting our own god.

A list of God's known attributes would fill a chapter, and then some. One of the most dominant characteristics in both Old and New Testaments is His holiness. In creation, we see His infinite power and wisdom. It is interesting that in this theme scripture of Jeremiah 9, God does not speak of His holiness, power or wisdom, or any other of his infinite qualities. Rather, He speaks of some of His attributes that relate specifically to His interaction with men.

God's Lovingkindness
His first characteristic is *steadfast love*, also translated *lovingkindness*. Life is not always kind to us. We might harbor questions about a God who would permit unkindness such as ones we have known. We don't understand how the details of life augment God's ultimate purposes, but His word assures us that our hardships are temporary. Furthermore, He tells us that our hardships in this life fit us for a greater weight of glory in the future. Jesus suffered, so if we suffer without losing faith, we share in fellowship with his suffering and will more fervently rejoice in our shared glory. In this passage, He assures us that His direct disposition toward us is love and kindness, even when we can't see it. What He requires of us is submissive faith that will blossom into an eternal love relationship with Him. Foremost, He wants us to know that He is a God of loving kindness. In His word, He gives us examples of love to follow and gives commands to love one another, for in this He delights.

This does not mean that everything that happens in this life is caused directly by His lovingkindness. We must know and understand that evil exists in the world. Evil causes bad things to happen. This simple truth is misunderstood by many in Christendom, causing them to ascribe all happenings to God and labeling them as 'God's will.' It is true that God brought a curse on this world because of sin, so in the big picture, He allows sin to reign for a season. Yet He has a larger purpose for not ending evil right now. Jesus told a parable that speaks to this very issue in the following parable:

Matthew 13:24-30 (NKJV)
[24] Another parable He put forth to them, saying: "The kingdom of heaven is like a man who sowed good seed in his field; [25] but while men slept, his enemy came and sowed tares among the wheat and went his way. [26] But when the grain had sprouted and produced a crop, then the tares also appeared. [27] So the servants of the owner came and said to him, 'Sir, did you not sow good seed in your field? How then does it have tares?' [28] He said to them, 'An enemy has done this.' The servants said to him, 'Do you want us then to go and gather them up?' [29] But he said, 'No, lest while you gather up the tares you also uproot the wheat

with them. ³⁰ *Let both grow together until the harvest, and at the time of harvest I will say to the reapers, "First gather together the tares and bind them in bundles to burn them, but gather the wheat into my barn."*

Note the phrase, *an enemy has done this*. God wants us to distinguish individual episodes of evil as not coming from Himself, but as coming from the hand of Satan. To blame God for everything that comes along is to either make Him the author of evil or to deny the existence of evil altogether. Neither stance is correct. *An enemy has done this.* Satan is the author of evil in the world and in our hearts. Let us not insult God's loving nature by labeling everything as being His will. God can and has brought calamity upon people, including His people, for judgment. He must also satisfy His own truth nature which calls for holiness and justice. But we must understand that evil exists, but not everything that goes against our wishes is evil. We must differentiate good and evil.

His permitting tares to coexist with wheat is addressed in this parable. It is for the benefit of the wheat that He leaves the tares. We don't understand all there is to know about the purposes of God, but we are told that it is for the growth and health of the wheat. God uses evil for our ultimate benefit.

Still, the evil flourishing around us can easily obscure the goodness of God from our perception if we do not understand from scripture the kind of God He is. The Bible has hundreds of references to God's lovingkindness. Let's look at a sampling of some of them.

Psalm 25:6 (NKJV)
⁶ *Remember, O LORD, Your tender mercies and Your lovingkindnesses, For they are from of old.*

John 3:16 (NKJV)
¹⁶ *For God so loved the world that He gave His only begotten Son, that whoever believes in Him should not perish but have everlasting life.*

Ephesians 1:3-5 (NKJV)
³ *Blessed be the God and Father of our Lord Jesus Christ, who*

has blessed us with every spiritual blessing in the heavenly places in Christ, ⁴ just as He chose us in Him before the foundation of the world, that we should be holy and without blame before Him in love, ⁵ having predestined us to adoption as sons by Jesus Christ to Himself, according to the good pleasure of His will,

Ephesians 2:4-5 (NKJV)
⁴ But God, who is rich in mercy, because of His great love with which He loved us, ⁵ even when we were dead in trespasses, made us alive together with Christ (by grace you have been saved),

Titus 3:4-6 (NKJV)
⁴ But when the kindness and the love of God our Savior toward man appeared, ⁵ not by works of righteousness which we have done, but according to His mercy He saved us, through the washing of regeneration and renewing of the Holy Spirit, ⁶ whom He poured out on us abundantly through Jesus Christ our Savior,

Furthermore, we see in this parable that the coexistence of the wheat and tares is temporary. The curse remains for a time, but not eternally. The purpose of the curse is that sin may not last forever. Our eternal life with the Father and the Son will not always be marred by our sinful inclinations, but will give way to perfection in us and in our relationship with God. This promise motivates us to have faith and hope, attitudes that will not be needed in our perfection, but are extremely valuable to us in this present life. God is love. The Old Testament writers knew it.

Psalm 36:7 (NIV2011)
⁷ How priceless is your unfailing love, O God! People take refuge in the shadow of your wings.

Joel 2:13 (NIV2011)
¹³ Rend your heart and not your garments. Return to the LORD your God, for he is gracious and compassionate, slow to anger and abounding in love, and he relents from sending calamity.

Likewise, the New Testament writers recognized Jesus as the fulfillment of God's promised manifestation of His love.

> *Ephesians 2:4-5 (NIV2011)*
> [4] *But because of his great love for us, God, who is rich in mercy,* [5] *made us alive with Christ even when we were dead in transgressions—it is by grace you have been saved.*

> *1 John 3:1 (NIV2011)*
> [1] *See what great love the Father has lavished on us, that we should be called children of God! And that is what we are! The reason the world does not know us is that it did not know him.*

> *1 John 4:8-10 (NIV2011)*
> [8] *Whoever does not love does not know God, because God is love.* [9] *This is how God showed his love among us: He sent his one and only Son into the world that we might live through him.* [10] *This is love: not that we loved God, but that he loved us and sent his Son as an atoning sacrifice for our sins.*

> *1 John 4:16 (NIV2011)*
> [16] *And so we know and rely on the love God has for us. God is love. Whoever lives in love lives in God, and God in them.*

God's Justice
The second attribute He wants us to know about in Jeremiah 9 is that He is a just God. He loves justice and promises to one day bring to judgment all injustices.

We seem to have an innate sense of justice from our earliest years. Cheryl and I have two daughters. When very young they learned that they were loved. Something else soon became apparent. They both had a sense of justice before they were old enough to have been taught it as an abstract concept. "That's not fair" was a very early response to our discipline when neither would admit guilt in a situation in which we had to intervene. Even as adults, we don't like to see justice perverted. We know a crime deserves punishment. We want truth to prevail. That too is evidence of our being made in God's image. God is just.

We know that life is not fair. This realization posed a major problem for traditional Jewish theologians. They typically taught that if you were good, God would reward you with temporal blessings. If hardships came upon a person, it indicated God was judging him for some sin. Remember when Jesus healed the man born blind . . .

John 9:2-3 (NIV2011)
[2] *His disciples asked him, "Rabbi, who sinned, this man or his parents, that he was born blind?"* [3] *"Neither this man nor his parents sinned," said Jesus, "but this happened so that the works of God might be displayed in him.*

Jesus gives a reply that may raise more questions than answers, but he dismantles the direct cause-and-effect connection between hardship and one's standing before God. Much of what is addressed in the Old Testament 'wisdom literature' (Job, Psalms, Proverbs, Ecclesiastes, Song of Songs) recognizes the temporal injustices of life and helps rectify them from a divine perspective. For example, the entirety of Psalm 73, written by Asaph, wrestled with his personal struggle with this dilemma. Here are a few key excerpts from it:

Psalm 73:1-3,11,16-19,23-25 (NIV2011)
[1] *Surely God is good to Israel, to those who are pure in heart.* [2] *But as for me, my feet had almost slipped; I had nearly lost my foothold.* [3] *For I envied the arrogant when I saw the prosperity of the wicked. . .* [11] *They say, "How would God know? Does the Most High know anything?". . .* [16] *When I tried to understand all this, it troubled me deeply* [17] *till I entered the sanctuary of God; then I understood their final destiny.* [18] *Surely you place them on slippery ground; you cast them down to ruin.* [19] *How suddenly are they destroyed, completely swept away by terrors! . . .* [23] *Yet I am always with you; you hold me by my right hand.* [24] *You guide me with your counsel, and afterward you will take me into glory.* [25] *Whom have I in heaven but you? And earth has nothing I desire besides you.*

Reading the whole psalm better draws out the anguish in Asaph's struggle. So grueling was it to him that he almost lost his trust in God over it. The whole issue was resolved when Asaph came to the eternal perspective of the issue. When God revealed the eventual justification of all things, the problem was solved.

The message was that God was not the perpetrator of the injustices of life, but neither was He detached from their existence. He had a plan for dealing with injustice.

God admonishes His people to act justly in a world in which life is not not just, because our just behavior reflects His own character to the world around us. It shines out in contrast to the darkness of injustice. As we worship Him with our lives, just behavior is a prescribed priority protocol.

> *Proverbs 21:3 (NKJV)*
> *³ To do righteousness and justice Is more acceptable to the LORD than sacrifice.*
>
> *Micah 6:8 (NIV2011)*
> *⁸ He has shown you, O mortal, what is good. And what does the LORD require of you? To act justly and to love mercy and to walk humbly with your God.*
>
> *Colossians 4:1 (NKJV)*
> *¹ Masters, give your bondservants what is just and fair, knowing that you also have a Master in heaven.*

Justice has, at its essence, the idea of honesty. Here are a few out of dozens of such supporting verses.

> *Proverbs 16:11 (NKJV)*
> *¹¹ Honest weights and scales are the LORD'S; All the weights in the bag are His work.*
>
> *Jeremiah 22:17 (NIV2011)*
> *¹⁷ "But your eyes and your heart are set only on dishonest gain, on shedding innocent blood and on oppression and extortion."*
>
> *1 Timothy 3:8 (NIV2011)*
> *⁸ In the same way, deacons are to be worthy of respect, sincere, not indulging in much wine, and not pursuing dishonest gain.*

We are to practice honesty in personal and business matters. Pressures of the competitive world around us are constantly tempting us to compromise in this area. We must decide beforehand who we will serve, God or money. When we choose God, we must have the integrity to follow through with that conviction.

Another component of justice is that it is based on truth and equity, not giving preference to one person or the other.

> *Romans 2:2 (NKJV)*
> *² But we know that the judgment of God is according to truth against those who practice such things.*
>
> *Psalm 82:2-4 (NKJV)*
> *² How long will you judge unjustly, And show partiality to the wicked? Selah ³ Defend the poor and fatherless; Do justice to the afflicted and needy. ⁴ Deliver the poor and needy; Free them from the hand of the wicked.*

God's Righteousness
Finally, God declares Himself to be a God who exercises righteousness in the earth, and who delights in it. God always acts in a manner consistent with His own character. When it appears to us that He is acting contrary to what we expected of Him, it is because we cannot comprehend the ultimate end of the matter in all its details. God has given us commandments to guide our thinking and behavior into ways of righteousness.

Our current culture has undermined our sense of righteousness by redefining 'tolerance' to mean 'acceptance' and by denying the existence of absolutes. Yet, absolutes remain absolutely essential. We don't want gravity or aerodynamic principles to vary when we are in a plane. In the civic arena, absolutes are necessary as the basis of law and order. In the realm of the divine, God is absolute. Since we are made in His image, I believe that aspect of His nature is built into us in our conscience. We can certainly choose to ignore it, but not without internal tension. Righteousness is the practice of willing obedience to revealed absolute truth. He delights in our righteous behavior because He Himself is righteous.

> *Psalm 7:17 (NIV2011)*
> *¹⁷ I will give thanks to the LORD because of his righteousness; I will sing the praises of the name of the LORD Most High.*

Psalm 9:8 (NIV2011)
⁸ He rules the world in righteousness and judges the peoples with equity.

Isaiah 45:8 (NIV2011)
⁸ "You heavens above, rain down my righteousness; let the clouds shower it down. Let the earth open wide, let salvation spring up, let righteousness flourish with it; I, the LORD, have created it.

God is righteousness. It rains down from His own nature. He looks for it among His people.

2 Kings 12:2 (NIV2011)
² Joash did what was right in the eyes of the LORD all the years Jehoiada the priest instructed him.

Matthew 5:6,10 (NIV2011)
⁶ Blessed are those who hunger and thirst for righteousness, for they will be filled . . . ¹⁰ Blessed are those who are persecuted because of righteousness, for theirs is the kingdom of heaven.

Matthew 6:33 (NIV2011)
³³ But seek first his kingdom and his righteousness, and all these things will be given to you as well.

Romans 1:17 (NIV2011)
¹⁷ For in the gospel the righteousness of God is revealed—a righteousness that is by faith from first to last, just as it is written: "The righteous will live by faith."

Romans 14:17 (NIV2011)
¹⁷ For the kingdom of God is not a matter of eating and drinking, but of righteousness, peace and joy in the Holy Spirit,

Summarizing Our Quest
Lovingkindness, justice and righteousness. The Bible is full of references to these qualities in regard to God's nature. He awaits the day when these shall prevail flawlessly in His people. Until then, He cherishes our efforts at them for His name's sake.

Psalm 33:5 (NIV2011)
⁵ The LORD loves righteousness and justice; the earth is full of his unfailing love.

If we would attempt to pattern our lives after God's nature, whom we cannot see, how do we do that? Jesus is the visible image of the invisible God. Therefore, followers of Jesus Christ are summoned to seek after one specific life goal. That goal is to become like Jesus in his character attributes.

Romans 8:29 (NKJV)
²⁹ For whom He foreknew, He also predestined to be conformed to the image of His Son, that He might be the firstborn among many brethren.

What attributes of Jesus are we seeking to replicate? We are not seeking to be like Him in His infinite attributes such as His power and wisdom. We are not seeking to compete for His place of honor and authority in heaven as Satan did. We don't covet His preeminence. But we are seeking to be like Him in the attributes that will allow us to be a worthy bride. We want to be like Him in a way that permits an eternal love relationship to flourish. These are the attributes that characterize certain facets of God's nature in our theme passage Jeremiah 9:23-24. It is our relationship with the God who has revealed Himself in scripture about which we boast. These three attributes listed in our theme passage are not the only attributes we are to emulate in seeking Christlikeness. They summarize the character of God for us. A longer list of specific attributes describing Christlikeness could be made by considering New Testament listings known as *the fruit of the Spirit*.

Galatians 5:22-23 (NIV2011)
²² But the fruit of the Spirit is love, joy, peace, forbearance, kindness, goodness, faithfulness, ²³ gentleness and self-control. Against such things there is no law.

Ephesians 5:9 (NIV2011)
⁹ (for the fruit of the light consists in all goodness, righteousness and truth)

Philippians 1:9-11 (NIV2011)
⁹ And this is my prayer: that your love may abound more and more in knowledge and depth of insight, ¹⁰ so that you may be able to discern what is best and may be pure and blameless for the day of Christ, ¹¹ filled with the fruit of righteousness that comes through Jesus Christ—to the glory and praise of God.

James 3:17-18 (NIV2011)
¹⁷ But the wisdom that comes from heaven is first of all pure; then peace-loving, considerate, submissive, full of mercy and good fruit, impartial and sincere. ¹⁸ Peacemakers who sow in peace reap a harvest of righteousness.

Fruit-bearing depends on being connected to the source of the fruit's life-blood, to Christ himself. Using the imagery of a grape vine, Jesus taught his disciples their purpose; to bear fruit by staying securely attached to his power.

John 15:5 (NIV2011)
⁵ "I am the vine; you are the branches. If you remain in me and I in you, you will bear much fruit; apart from me you can do nothing.

<u>A Divine Enigma</u>
We see this magnanimous introduction of God presented early in the life of the Hebrew nation. When Moses spent forty days and nights on Mount Sinai in the immediate presence and glory of God, while receiving the stone tablets carved by God with Ten Commandments, the Lord told him:

Exodus 34:6-7 (NKJV)
⁶ And the LORD passed before him and proclaimed, "The LORD, the LORD God, merciful and gracious, longsuffering, and abounding in goodness and truth, ⁷ keeping mercy for thousands, forgiving iniquity and transgression and sin, by no means clearing the guilty, visiting the iniquity of the fathers upon the children and the children's children to the third and the fourth generation."

This passage seems, at first reading, to contradict itself. God first portrays Himself as One who forgives, who is merciful. Then He says He does not clear the guilty and visits the sins of Fathers against their children and grandchildren. This dilemma reminds us of John's description of Jesus as being *full of grace and truth*. Grace and truth are strange partners in this phrase of John's. They seem like two diametrically polarizing characteristics. As a human, if I am an uncompromising advocate for truth, I may be lacking in grace. Or, perhaps, I am such a pacifist that I seem very gracious, but am short on conviction concerning truth claims. We find it very difficult to perfectly merge these two character qualities. Yet to Moses, God portrayed Himself in that manner and John declared it of Jesus. Grace. Truth.

Likewise, our theme passage Jeremiah 9:24 summarizes this part of God's character as *steadfast love, justice and righteousness*. Steadfast love seems to fall on the 'grace' side of God's character and seems incongruent with justice and righteousness which fall on the 'truth' side. This eventual coming together of seeming opposing excellencies was prophetically foreseen by the psalmist, prophetically peering into the redemptive future:

Psalm 85:10 (NKJV)
[10] Mercy and truth have met together; Righteousness and peace have kissed.

The psalmist saw a coming together of grace and truth. The emphasis in our Jeremiah passage is placed on characterizing God Himself. We can stretch our minds to comprehend that God perfectly combines them in his character.

However, note that last little phrase, *for in these I delight*. It sends a gentle, yet intent message that His delight in these attributes occurs when He sees them reflected in us. Can mere mortals do this? It was accomplished in the life of Jesus. That is the messianic message of Psalm 85. If we can approach Christ-likeness, we can exhibit this meeting and kissing of his attributes which became polarizing at the time of the fall of man. In this life, as we are being sanctified, we should be moving in that direction, recognizing that we approach it imperfectly. Our hope is in the day when we are glorified and the imperfection will become perfect.

Yet, that phrase *for in these I delight* should catch our attention. As His children, we should be eager to please our Father. There is no mystery here. He makes it perfectly clear. These attributes must ultimately characterize us if we are to spend an eternity as his bride, and they will be imputed to us in perfection at the time of our glorification. Yet, He longs to see them becoming reality in this present life, within our personal character and behavior. That is the intention of this phrase--to propel us to desire these attributes in ourselves because of our great esteem for our Father. That is why in our Christian walk, we strive to be Christ-like. We seek that because, as children of God, we know that is what delights our heavenly Father.

The Reconciliation of Grace and Truth in Salvation
Just how are grace and truth merged in the mind of God? How is it that the psalmist could say, *righteousness and peace have kissed*? How could God tell Moses that He was . . . *merciful and gracious, longsuffering, and abounding in goodness and truth,* [7] *keeping mercy for thousands, forgiving iniquity and transgression and sin, by no means clearing the guilty . . . ?* How can He practice *lovingkindness* alongside *justice and righteousness,* as expressed in our theme passage. How can these polar ideals be reconciled in the lives of God's people? This would be a haunting and unanswerable question if we were left to understand it using human logic. It would appear to be a contradiction from the perspective of a secular mindset.

God's profound solution to this question is found in the death of Jesus on the cross. He gave Himself in the person of Jesus as an atoning sacrifice for your sins and mine. Thus, He was not clearing the guilty, but instead paid that sin debt in full with His own sacrificial death. Jesus' death was a substitution. God substituted his sinless life for your hopeless one, thus satisfying His righteous and just nature, His truth nature. Simultaneously, in Jesus' death, God exercised His mercy and His grace nature toward sinners. His whole nature, both aspects of it, were satisfied at the cross.

In his substitutionary role, at the instant Christ took your sins upon himself, something else happened.

2 Corinthians 5:21 (ESV)
²¹ For our sake he made him to be sin who knew no sin, so that in him we might become the righteousness of God.

Not only did He put your sins on Christ, but He put Jesus' righteousness on you. On the cross, Jesus exchanged spiritual conditions with you. Now, when God looks upon you, He sees not your flaws, shortcomings and sins, but the perfect righteousness of Jesus with which He has clothed you. This describes our legal 'position' in the kingdom of heaven. Since our sins were already judged and punished at the cross, we no longer need to fear judgment in regard to salvation. God is just. He would not judge your sins twice.

In this chapter we have seen the nature of God. We discussed the divine relationship we can experience in correctly knowing the God of glory. We considered that we can have such a relationship by getting to know Him as he is, as He has revealed Himself to us. He has made Himself known to us in His creation, through scriptural accounts of His special self-revelation, through His Son, through answered prayer and the witness of His Spirit. We have discussed the immeasurable value of such a relationship. We focused on God's nature. We have briefly touched on the theology of knowing God.

If you are reading this book, but have never formed such a relationship with God and with Jesus, then you may be wondering how to begin. In chapter 7 we will consider a practical biblical path to knowing God in a redeeming way.

Chapter 6
OTHER THINGS WORTH BOASTING ABOUT

Since God is so all encompassing, any of His attributes are a worthy subject for boasting. In the previous chapter, we discussed that not only are God's essential, infinite characteristics worth boasting of, but also His relational attributes are worthy. We should boast in His lovingkindness, his justice and His righteousness.

However, even in this, we should be careful when boasting of the Lord, that our boast is truly in Him, and not a way to exalt ourselves indirectly by showing off His favor in us. For example, Paul was careful not to portray himself as deserving of praise when telling of the Lord's working through him. He went out of the way to show the great extent of God's grace in justifying even himself, the *worst of sinners*:

> 1 Timothy 1:13-16 (NKJV)
> [13] *although I was formerly a blasphemer, a persecutor, and an insolent man; but I obtained mercy because I did it ignorantly in unbelief.* [14] *And the grace of our Lord was exceedingly abundant, with faith and love which are in Christ Jesus.* [15] *This is a faithful saying and worthy of all acceptance, that Christ Jesus came into the world to save sinners, of whom I am chief.* [16] *However, for this reason I obtained mercy, that in me first Jesus Christ might show all longsuffering, as a pattern to those who are going to believe on Him for everlasting life.*

It is very easy to become smug in our piety; to use God's grace to lift ourselves up. When we tell someone we are praying for them, is it to build hope in God within the person being told, or is it a subtle attempt to ingratiate ourselves to that person? It is appropriate to let someone know we are praying for them, but we should be quick to exalt the Lord when He answers prayers, not taking partial credit for praying. It is the Lord who called us to pray and Him alone who answers those prayers in accordance with His plan and purpose.

In addition to boasting about God and His specific characteristics, scripture also speaks of other instances being appropriate of boasting. Even those things are valid objects of boast only because they point to the working of God in a situation or person. Thus, such boasting is directed toward God, even as we name a person or situation. Following are examples of such objects of boast.

Boasting of Others
One area of boasting that is supported in scripture is boasting of another person. Jesus boasted about the faith of a Gentile centurion:

Matthew 8:10 (NKJV)
[10] When Jesus heard it, He marveled, and said to those who followed, "Assuredly, I say to you, I have not found such great faith, not even in Israel!

If a person's actions are indeed praiseworthy, and if the motive is purely complimentary and not self-serving flattery, then praise of another is appropriate. In this manner, Paul often boasted of people in his care. He was interested in seeing them be built up in the faith.

2 Thessalonians 1:4 (ESV)
[4] Therefore we ourselves boast about you in the churches of God for your steadfastness and faith in all your persecutions and in the afflictions that you are enduring.

2 Corinthians 7:4 (ESV)
[4] I am acting with great boldness toward you; I have great pride in you; I am filled with comfort. In all our affliction, I am overflowing with joy.

Paul took great pride and joy in his intimate and rich relationship with the people of the churches he founded. But notice that even as he boasted about them, he was really boasting of the mighty transformation the Lord was making in them. His boast was in the Lord.

2 Corinthians 9:1-2 (ESV)
[1] Now it is superfluous for me to write to you about the ministry for the saints, [2] for I know your readiness, of which I boast about you to the people of Macedonia, saying that Achaia has

been ready since last year. And your zeal has stirred up most of them.

> 2 Corinthians 1:13-14 (ESV)
> [13] For we are not writing to you anything other than what you read and understand and I hope you will fully understand— [14] just as you did partially understand us—that on the day of our Lord Jesus you will boast of us as we will boast of you.

Those saints were evidence to Paul of God's grace being poured out through him. Both he and they could testify that it was only by grace they were in the family of God, so their boast was really in the Lord. Paul expressed this very thing to the church in Rome:

> Romans 15:17-18 (ESV)
> [17] In Christ Jesus, then, I have reason to be proud of my work for God. [18] For I will not venture to speak of anything except what Christ has accomplished through me to bring the Gentiles to obedience—by word and deed,

Furthermore, Paul's boast in the faith of the Corinthians was given as evidence against the Judaizers, a sect among the Jews who were trying to undermine Christianity by infiltrating Jewish rituals and customs into the gospel of grace. Their transformed lives and steadfast faith gave testimony to the operation of the Holy Spirit in the lives of the Corinthians.

> 2 Corinthians 5:12 (ESV)
> [12] We are not commending ourselves to you again but giving you cause to boast about us, so that you may be able to answer those who boast about outward appearance and not about what is in the heart.

Boasting in the Grace of God
This introduces us to the greatest things to boast about. God's grace is worthy of pride and worthy of boasts. Paul often boasted in God's work of grace at work within him:

> Philippians 2:14-16 (ESV)
> [16] holding fast to the word of life, so that in the day of Christ I may be proud that I did not run in vain or labor in vain.

James allows boasting from the recipients of God's grace, both lowly and rich:

> *James 1:9-10 (ESV)*
> *⁹ Let the lowly brother boast in his exaltation, ¹⁰ and the rich in his humiliation, because like a flower of the grass he will pass away.*

He implies that the lowly person has nothing in himself to boast about, but his boast is in the grace of God that exalts him in Christ. James further implies that the rich person comes to the realization of the futility of riches in the eternal quest and is therefore humbled by God's grace, rejoicing in it. Biblical examples of these are Matthew (Levi) in Mark 2:14-17, the sinful woman in Luke 7:36-50 and Zacchaeus in Luke 19:1-10.

Paul boasted in the grace of God poured out to himself, made manifest in his own weakness.

> *2 Corinthians 12:5-10 (ESV)*
> *⁵ On behalf of this man I will boast, but on my own behalf I will not boast, except of my weaknesses— ⁶ though if I should wish to boast, I would not be a fool, for I would be speaking the truth; but I refrain from it, so that no one may think more of me than he sees in me or hears from me. ⁷ So to keep me from becoming conceited because of the surpassing greatness of the revelations, a thorn was given me in the flesh, a messenger of Satan to harass me, to keep me from becoming conceited. ⁸ Three times I pleaded with the Lord about this, that it should leave me. ⁹ But he said to me, "My grace is sufficient for you, for my power is made perfect in weakness." Therefore I will boast all the more gladly of my weaknesses, so that the power of Christ may rest upon me. ¹⁰ For the sake of Christ, then, I am content with weaknesses, insults, hardships, persecutions, and calamities. For when I am weak, then I am strong.*

Weakness is not itself extoled as a virtue nor a worthy object of boasting. But when a *thorn . . . in the flesh* was given to Paul to derail his pride, it led to greater divine dependency, and to greater divine usefulness and that was cause to boast. When we become dependent, our weakness can serve to display the grace and glory of God. The ability for this to happen often rests in the attitude of the afflicted. One's mindset regarding life circumstances can either bring glory to God through his unwavering trust in God or call to question God's very character through his discontent. Thus, it is our response to hardship that allows God's purpose to be accomplished, as with Paul. When those same attitudes about our weaknesses are reflected in us, there is an unspoken boast about God. Contentment in the face of weakness can be a witness to God's grace at work in us.

Furthermore, our thorns in the flesh in this life can be avenues of spiritual blessing when they cause us to focus on eternity. Our weakness can be instrumental in the building of hope. It creates a yearning for future relief and an expectation of future glory as it trains us to *set our hearts on things above, not on earthly things.*

As we consider the grace of God, we find His promises at the heart of it. Promises of God are worthy topics for boasting. Redemption begins and is fulfilled in the Lord.

> *Romans 9:24-26 (NKJV)*
> *[24] even us whom He called, not of the Jews only, but also of the Gentiles? [25] As He says also in Hosea: "I will call them My people, who were not My people, And her beloved, who was not beloved." [26] "And it shall come to pass in the place where it was said to them, 'You are not My people,' There they shall be called sons of the living God."*

> *1 Peter 2:9-10 (NKJV)*
> *[9] But you are a chosen generation, a royal priesthood, a holy nation, His own special people, that you may proclaim the praises of Him who called you out of darkness into His marvelous light; [10] who once were not a people but are now the people of God, who had not obtained mercy but now have obtained mercy.*

The apostles extended this call from God as being not just a general, group call, but as being a personal call. Not only are we a holy nation, but we are now family with God!

John 1:12-13 (NKJV)
[12] But as many as received Him, to them He gave the right to become children of God, to those who believe in His name: [13] who were born, not of blood, nor of the will of the flesh, nor of the will of man, but of God.

Ephesians 2:19-22 (NKJV)
[19] Now, therefore, you are no longer strangers and foreigners, but fellow citizens with the saints and members of the household of God, [20] having been built on the foundation of the apostles and prophets, Jesus Christ Himself being the chief corner stone, [21] in whom the whole building, being joined together, grows into a holy temple in the Lord, [22] in whom you also are being built together for a dwelling place of God in the Spirit.

Chapter 7
BECOMING BOASTERS

Who are the boasters in the Lord? They are those men and women, boys and girls who know God and Jesus well enough to have a relationship with them. They value them enough to boast about them. These have eternal life through that divine relationship.

John 17:3 (ESV)
³ And this is eternal life, that they know you the only true God, and Jesus Christ whom you have sent.

In chapter 4, we discussed this concept of relationship with our Creator. We recognized that we would know little about Him if He had not chosen to reveal Himself to us. Knowledge unto salvation comes by hearing the good news about God's grace, and receiving it with gladness. For us, the propagation of such knowledge is through scripture. God may reveal Himself in other ways, but salvation knowledge comes from His recorded message which we read or hear, and in embracing it as truth. We comprehended the incalculable value of knowing God because of how wonderful He is and because it is for eternity. Eternity is too long to be wrong in this matter.

We cannot dismiss this topic by leaving it as an academic exercise. It does require the engagement of the intellect. Yet it is much more. It requires that the will of the person reading or hearing the message becoming engaging, seeking and following. If you have been reading this and have concluded that you do not have such a relationship; if you long to have this relationship or long to long for such relationship, then this chapter is for you.

Now we will seek to present a biblical path forward for an interested reader. Salvation is a relationship, as we have discussed. We are not trying to reduce it to a formula or ritual. Mainly, it is about adopting acceptable attitudes and embracing the truths of scripture about God and about Jesus. To lead us along a biblical path, scripture gives us some practical steps to follow. They are simple, but profound. We cannot ignore them in favor of a self-styled approach to God. We must follow them. Here is what scripture teaches.

His Perspective, His Terms

Everyone has an opinion about God and eternal life. If they believe in it, they have an opinion about how to achieve it. Our first truth that must be adopted is to recognize that our opinions don't change the reality that it is outside our control and we have nothing to say about it. God alone gets to define eternal life and to set its course. God has revealed Himself and His criteria for salvation in His written word, the Bible. We cannot add or detract from it. We can pull out passages and principles from it that are specific to achieving salvation and that is what we are going to do now.

Recognize God is Holy and You are Not

God has set a standard for holiness. It is perfect righteousness with no exceptions. This standard is necessary because that is the nature of God Himself. He is perfectly holy. To be in His presence requires that same characteristic. You, and every other human ever born, except Jesus, have failed at this criterion.

> *Romans 3:10-12 (ESV)*
> *[10] as it is written: "None is righteous, no, not one; [11] no one understands; no one seeks for God. [12] All have turned aside; together they have become worthless; no one does good, not even one."*

A person seeking salvation must recognize that he is both hopeless to achieve it through his own efforts, his own merit and that he is helpless to remedy his own hopeless condition. Only when we see the utter depravity in which we dwell, only then can we be prepared to hear God's solution. There is no solution within the unredeemed heart. That solution must come from outside yourself. Conviction of sin comes from reading or hearing scripture.

> *Romans 3:20 (ESV)*
> *[20] For by works of the law no human being will be justified in his sight, since through the law comes knowledge of sin.*

The Law, any law, any set of rules such as the Ten Commandments, are for the conviction of the sinner. They are not given as a way to salvation since no one is able to keep them. They, in themselves, leave the sinner in condemnation.

Repent of Sin
Recognizing that your sinfulness makes you an enemy of God should prompt repentance. Repentance is being genuinely sorry for your sins. But it is much more than that. It involves a desire to turn away from sin and turn to God. It involves an intentional commitment to pursue righteousness.

> *Matthew 4:17 (ESV)*
> *17 From that time Jesus began to preach, saying, "Repent, for the kingdom of heaven is at hand."*
>
> *Mark 1:14-15 (ESV)*
> *14 Now after John was arrested, Jesus came into Galilee, proclaiming the gospel of God, 15 and saying, "The time is fulfilled, and the kingdom of God is at hand; repent and believe in the gospel."*
>
> *Acts 3:17-19 (ESV)*
> *17 "And now, brothers, I know that you acted in ignorance, as did also your rulers. 18 But what God foretold by the mouth of all the prophets, that his Christ would suffer, he thus fulfilled. 19 Repent therefore, and turn back, that your sins may be blotted out,*

Jesus is the Way, the Only Way
Early in scripture, as early as Genesis 3, we are introduced to the concept of a Messiah. The prophets spoke specifically about him. Special occasions in the life of God's chosen nation Israel spoke of him in historic imagery. He was symbolized in Hebrew worship practices. The covenants pointed to him. By the time of Jesus' birth, there existed an air of messianic expectation among the Jewish people. Prophetic timelines seemed to converge for such fulfillment. People were fully aware that their only hope was a divine intervention, so they anticipated their Messiah.

Yet, because of their own selfish prejudices and ambitions, Jesus did not match the messiah they were looking for. Instead of embracing him as their Messiah, they killed him. Three days later, God raised him from the tomb. All of this was according to the plan of God. Even the details had been prophesied long before. Jesus died as a substitute for you and me who deserved to die. Based on his anticipated sacrificial death:

John 14:6 (ESV)
⁶ Jesus said to him, "I am the way, and the truth, and the life. No one comes to the Father except through me.

Later, Peter and John stood before the Jewish council after healing a lame beggar in the name of Jesus and testified:

Acts 4:10,12 (ESV)
¹⁰ let it be known to all of you and to all the people of Israel that by the name of Jesus Christ of Nazareth, whom you crucified, whom God raised from the dead—by him this man is standing before you well . . . ¹² And there is salvation in no one else, for there is no other name under heaven given among men by which we must be saved."

Jesus was who he said he was—God in flesh. He proved it by being raised from the dead. He alone is the acceptable substitute for us in atoning for sins. No other religion looks to a leader who dares to even make this claim. No other religious leader is, or has been, our substitute. This is the truly radical, unique, exclusive, exceptional, distinctive message of Christianity.

Believe Jesus Died and Rose from the Dead for You

Believing this truth, that Jesus is indeed God in flesh and that he gave his life a ransom for you—that is your part in salvation. This level of believing is called "saving faith."

John 3:16 (ESV)
¹⁶ "For God so loved the world, that he gave his only Son, that whoever believes in him should not perish but have eternal life.

John 3:18 (ESV)
¹⁸ Whoever believes in him [Jesus] is not condemned, but whoever does not believe is condemned already, because he has not believed in the name of the only Son of God.

Believing is the key response to biblical truth regarding eternal life. This kind of believing hears the message and by way of it, desires to enter into God's 'family'. Specifically, what core belief must be understood and believed? We are not called to believe in some abstract or ambiguous cloud of ideas to be saved. The content of that belief is very distinct, very clear, very simple. It is believing that Jesus is God. It is understanding that he gave his own life as a substitute for you. It is embracing Jesus as both Lord and Savior.

Confess Jesus as Lord and Savior

Saving faith must embrace Jesus as both Lord and Savior. As a corollary to believing, scripture says we must confess that specific belief. We must believe it strongly enough to give outward confession to it.

> *Romans 10:9-10 (ESV)*
> *[9] because, if you confess with your mouth that Jesus is Lord and believe in your heart that God raised him from the dead, you will be saved. [10] For with the heart one believes and is justified, and with the mouth one confesses and is saved.*

This passage, along with many others, sets forth the core belief that Jesus must be believed and embraced as both Lord and Savior. It tells us something else. It stresses that the intellectual belief must be nailed down with an outward confession of the specific constitution of that belief.

Identify with Jesus in Water Baptism

Another witness of believing Jesus is Lord and Savior that is commanded in scripture is to embrace that belief for yourself and identify with it through baptism. Baptism is translated from the original Greek word meaning to immerse or submerge. In biblical baptism, the person is momentarily immersed in a bath of water by another believer in the name of God the Father, the Son and the Holy Spirit. The death, burial and resurrection of Jesus are symbolized in the immersion and emergence of a believer. That is how we are called to identify with Jesus. Baptism further symbolizes the death of the old sin nature of the believer and the rising to new life. In baptism, we put our transformation from death to life alongside Jesus' resurrected life.

> *Romans 6:3-4 (ESV) [3]*
> *Do you not know that all of us who have been baptized into*

Christ Jesus were baptized into his death? ⁴ We were buried therefore with him by baptism into death, in order that, just as Christ was raised from the dead by the glory of the Father, we too might walk in newness of life.

Colossians 2:12-14 (ESV)
¹² having been buried with him in baptism, in which you were also raised with him through faith in the powerful working of God, who raised him from the dead. ¹³ And you, who were dead in your trespasses and the uncircumcision of your flesh, God made alive together with him, having forgiven us all our trespasses, ¹⁴ by canceling the record of debt that stood against us with its legal demands. This he set aside, nailing it to the cross.

The same power of God that raised Jesus will also raise up a new creation in us. This baptism is done at the instruction of Jesus.

Matthew 28:18-20 (ESV)
¹⁸ And Jesus came and said to them, "All authority in heaven and on earth has been given to me. ¹⁹ Go therefore and make disciples of all nations, baptizing them in the name of the Father and of the Son and of the Holy Spirit, ²⁰ teaching them to observe all that I have commanded you. And behold, I am with you always, to the end of the age."

This 'great commission' is a call to make disciples. How? Two main thrusts are summarized: 1) initiation into faith, represented here by one's submission in baptism, and 2) teaching believers how to submit to Jesus' lordship, an ongoing education. The apostles preached that same message about baptism:

Acts 2:37-39 (ESV)
³⁷ Now when they [the listening Jews] *heard this they were cut to the heart, and said to Peter and the rest of the apostles, "Brothers, what shall we do?" ³⁸ And Peter said to them, "Repent and be baptized every one of you in the name of Jesus Christ for the forgiveness of your sins, and you will receive the gift of the Holy Spirit. ³⁹ For the promise is for you and for your children and for all who are far off, everyone whom the Lord our God calls to himself."*

In Summary

These steps are about initiation into the Christian faith. Done with pure motive and with eager obedience, this initiation introduces you into the family of God. It qualifies you to be a boaster. May we become boasters in the glory of God. And in the salvation of God. May our boast always be in the Lord. He alone is worthy of such boasting. He is worthy because of His greatness, His supremacy, His lovingkindness, His justice, His righteousness. He is worthy because of His mercy and grace which He has poured out upon us and continues to pour upon us. Between initiation into saving faith and the reward of living in the realized presence of God for eternity, there is a time of growing in knowledge and deepening of the relationship in this life. We who are redeemed will spend eternity boasting of the Lord in everlasting worship. As for now, when we stand and sing hymns and choruses, may they be our eternity-focused boast in the Lord.

May our boasting draw others to God and to Jesus, our Lord. Jesus' final words were about taking our boast of God and of himself to the whole world. God's purpose is to populate heaven with people who will spend their eternal lives in relationship with Him. Together we will spend eternity boasting of Him in the courts of the angels, with ecstatic joy. John described such a scene from his vision of the Revelation:

> *Revelation 5:6-14 (NKJV)*
> *[6] And I looked, and behold, in the midst of the throne and of the four living creatures, and in the midst of the elders, stood a Lamb as though it had been slain, having seven horns and seven eyes, which are the seven Spirits of God sent out into all the earth. [7] Then He came and took the scroll out of the right hand of Him who sat on the throne. [8] Now when He had taken the scroll, the four living creatures and the twenty-four elders fell down before the Lamb, each having a harp, and golden bowls full of incense, which are the prayers of the saints. [9] And they sang a new song, saying: "You are worthy to take the scroll, And to open its seals; For You were slain, And have redeemed us to God by Your blood Out of every tribe and tongue and people and nation, [10] And have made us kings and priests to our*

God; And we shall reign on the earth." [11] Then I looked, and I heard the voice of many angels around the throne, the living creatures, and the elders; and the number of them was ten thousand times ten thousand, and thousands of thousands, [12] saying with a loud voice: "Worthy is the Lamb who was slain To receive power and riches and wisdom, And strength and honor and glory and blessing!" [13] And every creature which is in heaven and on the earth and under the earth and such as are in the sea, and all that are in them, I heard saying: "Blessing and honor and glory and power Be to Him who sits on the throne, And to the Lamb, forever and ever!" [14] Then the four living creatures said, "Amen!" And the twenty-four elders fell down and worshiped Him who lives forever and ever.

Now that will be a boast. May it be your boast now.

www.ingramcontent.com/pod-product-compliance
Lightning Source LLC
Chambersburg PA
CBHW071408040426
42444CB00009B/2143